Nonfiction: Writing for Fact and Argument

Address delivered at the dedication of the Cemetery at Gettysburg.

Four score and seven years ago our fathers brought forth on this continent, a new nation, conceived in Liberty, and dedicated to the proposition that all men are created equal.

Now we are engaged in a great civil war, testing whether that nation, or any nation so conceived and so dedicated, can long endure. We are met on a great battle-field of that war. We have come to dedicate a portion of that field, as a final resting place for those who here gave their lives, that that nation might live. It is altogether fitting and proper that we should do this.

But, in a larger sense, we can not dedicate — we can not consecrate — we can not hallow — this ground. The brave men, living and dead, who struggled here, have consecrated it, far above our poor power to add

Effective Speeches

Valerie Bodden

CREATIVE EDUCATION

Published by Creative Education

P.O. Box 227, Mankato, Minnesota 56002

Creative Education is an imprint of The Creative Company

www.thecreativecompany.us

Design and art direction by Rita Marshall

Production by The Design Lab

Printed by Corporate Graphics in the United States of America

Photographs by Alamy (akg-images, The Art Gallery Collection, Mary Evans Picture Library), AP Images (Ron Edmonds), Corbis (Bettmann, Lake Country Museum), Getty Images (Alfred Eisenstaedt, Fox Photos, FPG, Liaison Agency, Travel Ink, US Air Force/Time & Life Pictures, Washington Bureau), iStockphoto (Don Bayley, Doug Cannell, Trevor Hunt, Tim Nichols, Kevin Russ)

Library of Congress Cataloging-in-Publication Data

Bodden, Valerie.

Effective speeches / by Valerie Bodden.

p. cm. — (Nonfiction: writing for fact and argument)

Includes bibliographical references and index.

Summary: An introduction to the ways that writers compose the content of speeches. Excerpts and analysis help to explain the importance of persuasiveness and spoken sound in this nonfiction form.

ISBN 978-1-58341-935-9

1. Speechwriting—Juvenile literature. 2. Public speaking—Juvenile literature. I. Title.

PN4142.B63 2010   808.5—dc22   2009024171

CPSIA: 120109 PO1094

First Edition

9 8 7 6 5 4 3 2 1

ONTENTS

Words surround us. They are printed on cereal boxes, across road signs, and in newspapers, books, and magazines. They are spoken, too—in the classroom, on television, at home. Sometimes words entertain us. Sometimes they teach us. Sometimes they persuade us. And sometimes they do all three. Some of the words that surround us weave a world of `fiction`*—in which the people and events are not real but are the product of another's imagination. Other words, though, form the fabric of real life. These words belong to the realm of* `nonfiction`*, and they tell us about what is happening in the world around us.*

When you hear the word "nonfiction," you may picture your history textbook or a hefty newspaper. But nonfiction can be—and often is—spoken as well. Think about all the times you've listened to teachers talk about photosynthesis or democracy, for example. What they are saying is nonfiction—it has to do with real life. Or think about your parents' lectures on respect and obedience. Those are nonfiction, too. So are speeches.

While your parents probably don't write out what they're going to say ahead of time, most speechwriters do. But when they write, they try to write as if they were speaking. They want to sound like themselves, not like some stiff, lifeless text on the page. At the same time, they want to make a clear, strong point. When they succeed in combining content and style, the result can be a speech that fills heads, moves hearts, or changes actions.

American civil rights leader
Martin Luther King Jr. (1929-68)

People have been writing and delivering speeches for thousands of years. As long ago as 2400 B.C., an Egyptian official named Ptahhotep offered advice for "fair speaking," encouraging speakers to avoid arguments with those wiser than themselves but to point out the evil in an argument given by someone considered an equal. Public speech was also important among the ancient Hebrews, and many of the speeches of their leaders, such as Moses and Samuel, are recorded in the Bible.

Beginning around 500 B.C., the art of oratory (public speaking) rose to prominence in ancient Greece, where the majority of speeches took place in courts of law and were focused on legal matters. Other speeches were political in nature, as citizens gathered to debate major issues. Some speeches were ceremonial, intended to pay tribute to an occasion, city, state, or person—especially a military figure who had fallen in battle.

In the fourth century B.C., the philosopher Aristotle wrote the text *Rhetoric*, in which he identified three techniques used to convince, or persuade, an audience: *ethos*, or credibility; *pathos*, or emotions; and *logos*, or logic. By the

end of the century, though, oratory had declined
in Greece. It was revived by the Romans two centuries later. Like Grecian speeches, most Roman
orations were political or legal in nature. Large
audiences often gathered in the courts of Rome's
public Forum to observe trials, in which orators
(serving in the roles of modern lawyers) often
used emotion, prejudice, and flowery speech to

The philosopher Aristotle
(384–322 B.C.)

win cases. In the more serious Senate, sound reasoning prevailed over an ornate style. During the first century B.C., Marcus Tullius Cicero became the leading orator in Rome. He established canons, or rules, of rhetoric focusing on a speech's arguments, arrangement, and style that are still followed today.

Marcus Tullius Cicero
delivering a speech

After Cicero's death in 43 B.C., oratory declined in Rome, but it rose again in the early Christian church in the form of the sermon. Oratory remained largely in the religious realm for more than 1,000 years, but the Renaissance of the 14th through 16th centuries brought a renewed interest in the rhetorical style of the ancient Greeks and Romans.

By the late 18th century, political speeches had again grown in importance, especially in the American colonies, where the desire for independence from Britain inspired impassioned speeches. The excerpt on the following page is from a speech delivered by American revolutionary Patrick Henry to the Second Virginia Convention in March 1775. In the speech, Henry argues that the colony should arm itself against the British. (Following the custom of the day, Henry addresses his remarks to the president of the Convention, whom he respectfully refers to as "sir.") As you read this excerpt, try to imagine what effect Henry's speech might have had on his listeners.

Has Great Britain any enemy in this quarter of the world to call for all this accumulation of navies and armies? No, sir, she has none. They are meant for us; they can be meant for no other.... And what have we to oppose them? Shall we try argument? Sir, we have been trying that for the last ten years.... Shall we resort to entreaty and humble supplication? What terms shall we find that have not been already exhausted? Let us not, I beseech you, sir, deceive ourselves longer. Sir, we have done everything that could be done to avert the storm which is now coming on.... There is no longer any room for hope. If we wish to be free ... we must fight!...

They tell us, sir, that we are weak—unable to cope with so formidable an adversary. But when shall we be stronger? Will it be the next week or the next year? Will it be when we are totally disarmed and when a British guard shall be stationed in every house? Shall we gather strength by irresolution and inaction?... Three millions of people armed in the holy cause of liberty, and in such a country as that which we possess, are invincible by any force which our enemy can send against us.... The war is inevitable—and let it come! I repeat, sir, let it come!...

Gentlemen may cry, peace, peace—but there is no peace. The war is actually begun!... Is life so dear, or peace so sweet, as to be purchased at the price of chains and slavery? Forbid it, Almighty God! I know not what course others may take but, as for me, give me liberty or give me death!

After Henry's speech, the Virginia Convention ultimately approved his call to arms against the British, and the American colonists fought for and won their independence, spurred on by orators such as Henry, along with James Otis, Samuel Adams, and Josiah Quincy. The late 1700s also saw the rise of oratory in Britain, especially in the ruling body of parliament, and in France, especially during the French Revolution.

During the 19th century, the focus of oratory shifted, as speakers turned from Aristotle's *Rhetoric* to theories written by George Campbell and Hugh Blair of Scotland. Campbell and Blair believed that speakers should appeal not only to reason and emotion but to experience and the imagination as well. As a result, many 19th-century speeches included stories to illustrate their point. (And stories remain an important part of many speeches today.)

The biggest change to oratory came about with the invention of radio and television in the 20th century, however. In the 1930s and '40s, U.S. president Franklin Roosevelt hosted "fireside chats," in which he spoke to millions of Americans over the radio, using the personable style of a

friendly talk. Television has also lent itself to a more conversational style of speaking, as well as to shorter speeches, often with a focus on phrases that will play well as sound bites . Today's global media also means that any speech has the potential to be seen by a worldwide audience. So watch a political campaign, listen to a sermon, or pay attention during a class lecture—you'll soon see that speeches are still a large part of how we get our information!

President Franklin
Roosevelt (1882–1945)

The world's truly great speeches, the ones that
live forever, are generally given by great leaders
on great occasions—the threat of war, the death
of a beloved person, or the response to a disaster.
In these cases, it is often the occasion as much
as the words spoken that makes a speech memorable.
This does not mean, however, that a speech given
by an ordinary person on an ordinary day cannot be
great; although your speech about the Declaration
of Independence may not be recorded in the history
books, it has the chance to live on in the minds of
your history classmates.

An artistic rendering of
the Hebrew leader Moses

Before you begin to write a speech, you must determine what your purpose in writing it is. Do you want to inform your audience about a subject? Do you hope to convince them to take some sort of action? Are you paying tribute to someone you admire? Answering such questions will help you figure out what kind of speech to write.

Informational speeches, as the name implies, are intended to give information to an audience. When your teacher stands in front of class and talks about the life and works of poet William Shakespeare, he or she is, in effect, giving an informational speech. In addition to giving facts about a subject, an informational speech can demonstrate a process, such as how to change a bike tire.

If, instead of giving information, you want to convince your listeners that what you believe is right, then you will give a persuasive speech. The goal of a persuasive speech is to reinforce or change your audience's thoughts or behavior. Ultimately, many persuasive speeches also call upon audience members to take some specific action. In order to persuade your listeners, you will likely rely on both reason (an appeal to the mind) and emotion (an appeal to the heart). Persuasive speaking generally requires a great deal of conviction—if audience members see that you are passionate about your cause, they may be moved to take action with you. Look back at Patrick Henry's persuasive speech on page 12. Notice the conviction he shows as he appeals to both his listeners' minds and hearts. It's hard to get more passionate than "Give me liberty or give me death!"

Informational and persuasive speeches can be given on any occasion, but some occasions call for special types of speeches. A graduation calls for a commencement speech, for example, and a wedding is usually celebrated with a toast. Tributes highlight the accomplishments of a person or commemorate an event. The eulogy is a special type of tribute intended to honor someone who has died. "Occasional speeches" need to fit the occasion for which they are given. You wouldn't likely speak of somber topics at a wedding or tell jokes at a funeral, for example (although you might use gentle humor in remembering the events of a person's life).

The following excerpt is from a eulogy given for John F. Kennedy Jr. by his uncle, Senator Edward "Teddy" Kennedy, on July 23, 1999. As you read, think about how the eulogy fits the occasion.

Once, when they asked John what he would do if he went into politics and was elected president, he said: "I guess the first thing is call up Uncle Teddy and gloat." I loved that. It was so like his father.

From the first day of his life, John seemed to belong not only to our family, but to the American family.

The whole world knew his name before he did.

A famous photograph showed John racing across the lawn as his father landed in the White House helicopter and swept up John in his arms. When my brother saw that photo, he exclaimed, "Every mother in the United States is saying, 'Isn't it wonderful to see that love between a son and his father, the way that John races to be with his father.' Little do they know—that son would have raced right by his father to get to that helicopter."

But John was so much more than those long ago images emblazoned in our minds. He was a boy who grew into a man with a zest for life and a love of adventure. He was a pied piper who brought us all along....

John was a serious man who brightened our lives with his smile and his grace....

He was still becoming the person he would be, and doing it by the beat of his own drummer. He had only just begun. There was in him a great promise of things to come....

We dared to think ... that this John Kennedy would live to comb gray hair, with his beloved [wife] Carolyn by his side. But like his father, he had every gift but length of years.

We who have loved him from the day he was born, and watched the remarkable man he became, now bid him farewell.

In his moving eulogy, Senator Kennedy doesn't present a biography of his nephew, giving us his history from his birth until his death in an airplane crash. Instead, he highlights the special qualities that made John F. Kennedy Jr. unique. He acknowledges Kennedy's powerful impact on the world and talks about the grief that the family feels at his untimely death. Although the eulogy is mournful, the senator also adds a touch of humor, speaking of his nephew's joke that if he were elected president, he would call his uncle to gloat. Such a lighthearted remembrance likely brought a smile to many grieving faces.

As you read this eulogy, how did you feel about John F. Kennedy Jr.? What do you think the senator's purpose was in giving this speech? Do you think he achieved it? When you write your next speech, think about your purpose. Then, whether you want to celebrate a life, congratulate a graduating class, inform a group, or move someone to action, put your pen to paper and give voice to your thoughts!

John F. Kennedy Jr. as a boy under his father's presidential desk

Building a Structure

Nearly any subject can serve as the topic for a speech, but you will usually be most successful if you choose a subject that interests you. After all, if you're bored by your topic, your audience likely will be, too. In fact, as you think about your topic, you should consider not only what interests you, but also what is likely to interest your audience members based on their age, occupation, education, and interests. Don't try to cover everything there is to say about your subject, either, no matter how interesting it is. You want to narrow your topic to one that can be discussed in the time allotted. If your subject is cars, for example, you might narrow it to how cars work, why one car is better than another, or the early history of automobile development.

Once you've narrowed your topic, you can begin to collect the information you will need to support your point. Sometimes, that information will come from your own head, especially if your speech is based on personal experience or skills. For many speeches, though, you will need to research your topic in books or other documents or through interviews with experts. The more you know about your subject, the more credible you will be as a speaker, and the more receptive the audience will likely be to your message.

Once you've gathered your information, you need to arrange it into a logical structure, usually consisting of an introduction, a body, and a conclusion. The introduction of a speech should grab the audience's attention, because if you don't get it at this point, you're not likely to gain it later on. It should also preview your speech and let listeners know why it is important—so important that they should give up their time to listen.

The body is the meat of your speech. It is where you make your point and prove it with supporting material. In general, a speech should focus on two or three main points. Too many more than that may be too much for listeners to remember—and you may not have time to address each point fully. Your points can be arranged in chronological order, spatial order (top to bottom, for example), order of importance, or any other logical fashion that makes your speech easy to follow.

Once you have made all of your points, don't just stop talking. Wrap up your speech with a

brief conclusion. This is the last impression the audience will have of you, so you want to be sure it summarizes your points and makes an impact on your listeners, perhaps with a powerful quote or a stirring call to action.

As you read the following excerpt from a speech by American suffragist Susan B. Anthony, pay careful attention to its structure. Also keep in mind that the speech was given in 1873, at a time when women were not allowed to vote.

Suffragist Susan B. Anthony (1820-1906)

I stand before you tonight under indictment for the alleged crime of having voted at the last presidential election, without having a lawful right to vote. It shall be my work this evening to prove to you that in thus voting, I not only committed no crime, but, instead, simply exercised my citizen's rights, guaranteed to me and all United States citizens by the National Constitution, beyond the power of any state to deny....

It was we, the people; not we, the white male citizens; nor yet we, the male citizens; but we, the whole people, who formed the Union. And we formed it, not to give the blessings of liberty, but to secure them ... to the whole people—women as well as men....

For any state to make sex a qualification that must ever result in the disfranchisement [denial of rights] of one entire half of the people is ... a violation of the supreme law of the land.... To [women] this government is not a democracy....

Webster, Worcester, and Bouvier all define a citizen to be a person in the United States, entitled to vote and hold office.

The only question left to be settled now is: Are women persons? And I hardly believe any of our opponents will have the hardihood to say they are not. Being persons, then, women are citizens....

We no longer petition Legislature or Congress to give us the right to vote. We appeal to women everywhere to exercise their too long neglected "citizen's right to vote."...

And it is on this line that we propose to fight our battle for the ballot—all peaceably, but nevertheless persistently through to complete triumph, when all United States citizens shall be recognized as equals before the law.

Did you notice how Anthony grabs our attention with the beginning of this speech? She shocks us by saying that she has been indicted, or charged, with a crime. Then she goes on to tell us exactly what she's going to do in her speech: prove that she committed no crime but instead exercised her rights as a citizen. In the body of her speech, she does just that. She shows that the country was formed by all people, not just by men. She shows how women's rights have been denied in the country, despite the fact that citizenship has been defined as being a "person," not a "man," living in the U.S. Since women are people, she reasons that women have the same voting rights as men.

As Anthony concludes her speech, she calls on women to exercise the right to vote that she has just proven they already have. Then she looks forward to a future "when all United States citizens shall be recognized as equal before the law." On this hopeful note, we are left feeling satisfied that Anthony has made her point and is done speaking. Your speech can make us feel that way too—just grab our attention, tell us something important, and then let us go into the world to do what we need to with our new information.

A suffragist heeding Susan
B. Anthony's call to action

THE SUFFRAGETTE

EDITED BY CHRISTABEL PANKHURST.

No. 2.   OCTOBER 25, 1912.   Price 1d.

AN

ANTI-SHOCK

BY

JAMES BARR

When making a speech, you can't simply state your point and leave it at that—or if you do, you're not likely to make much of an impression on your audience. You need to prove your point, and there are many ways to do so. Often, speeches need to relate information or explain an object, process, or idea. This is called exposition. Definitions and examples are types of exposition. Giving an audience a definition helps them understand exactly what you mean when you use a specific term, while examples can help illustrate a concept.

Sometimes the best way to support your point is to provide statistics. If your speech is about the growth in child abuse cases, for example, you will obviously need to provide statistics to prove that the problem of child abuse is, in fact, growing. At the same time, though, remember that your listeners are only hearing—and not seeing—the numbers you give, so don't use so many that you lose or confuse them. Whenever possible, try to illustrate numbers for your audience. If 1,000 children in your state are physically abused every year, for example, and that's also the population of your school, you could relate the two figures, perhaps asking your audience to imagine that every student in your school was the victim of physical abuse. This will help listeners picture exactly how many children the number 1,000 represents.

While exposition and statistics are often necessary to prove a point, they can be rather dry on their own. That's where narration and anecdotes come in. Stories can enliven your speech by bringing listeners directly into an event. Make sure that your story helps to prove your point, though; an unrelated story, no matter how interesting, will leave readers wondering why you told it. Description is another way to add interest to a speech. It allows you to show listeners something rather than simply telling them about it.

If your speech is persuasive, you have the extra burden of arguing your point. You can appeal to your listeners' reason to prove that what you would have them believe is true. An appeal to reason involves presenting evidence and showing how it supports a conclusion. You can also present the opinions of experts—often through a quote—which can lend credibility to your argument. And, since most people make decisions based on both their

head and their heart, you can appeal to the audience's emotions.

The following excerpt is from a speech given
by U.S. president Ronald Reagan on June 6, 1984,
at Pointe du Hoc, France, in commemoration of the
40th anniversary of D-Day (the Allied invasion of
German-occupied France during World War II). As
you read the excerpt, notice the various methods
Reagan uses to show the heroism of the men involved
in the invasion.

President Ronald Reagan
(1911–2004) at Pointe du Hoc

We stand on a lonely, windswept point on the northern shore of France. The air is soft, but 40 years ago at this moment, the air was dense with smoke and the cries of men, and the air was filled with the crack of rifle fire and the roar of cannon. At dawn, on the morning of the 6th of June, 1944, 225 Rangers jumped off the British landing craft and ran to the bottom of these cliffs. Their mission was one of the most difficult and daring of the invasion: to climb these sheer and desolate cliffs and take out the enemy guns....

The Rangers looked up and saw the enemy soldiers.... And the American Rangers began to climb. They shot rope ladders over the face of these cliffs and began to pull themselves up. When one Ranger fell, another would take his place. When one rope was cut, a Ranger would grab another and begin his climb again.... Two hundred and twenty-five came here. After 2 days of fighting, only 90 could still bear arms.

Behind me is a memorial that symbolizes the Ranger daggers that were thrust into the top of these cliffs. And before me are the men who put them there....

I think I know what you may be thinking right now—thinking "we were just part of a bigger effort; everyone was brave that day." Well, everyone was. Do you remember the story of Bill Millin of the 51st Highlanders? Forty years ago today, British troops were pinned down near a bridge, waiting desperately for help. Suddenly, they heard the sound of bagpipes, and some thought they were dreaming. Well, they weren't. They looked up and saw Bill Millin with his bagpipes, leading the reinforcements and ignoring the smack of the bullets into the ground around him.

Reagan's speech is certainly powerful, but why? He opens by showing us the scene at Pointe du Hoc, which he describes as "lonely" and "windswept," with air that is "soft." Then he takes us back to the scene 40 years earlier, when the cliffs echoed with the sounds of men and guns and smoke filled the air. He brings us further into the scene by narrating the events of that day, giving us a vision of U.S. Army Rangers struggling up the cliffs, only to be shot down and replaced by others.

In addition to description, Reagan also incorporates cold, hard numbers into his speech. He tells us that 225 Rangers stormed the cliffs, but only 90 were still capable of fighting 2 days later. In this case, the numbers need no interpretation; we can do the math: more than half of the Rangers involved in the invasion were either killed or seriously wounded. Finally, Reagan reminds us that the people involved in the invasion were not nameless, faceless soldiers; they were individuals like Bill Millin, who played his bagpipes as he led additional troops into the heart of the battle.

Allied planes bombing the French coast during World War II

Of course, not all speeches will be about events of such enormous significance—but all speeches do need to marshal the right supporting materials to make their point. So decide what it is about your subject that speaks to you—and then speak about it to your audience!

American soldiers during the D-Day invasion

When you speak, people notice not only *what* you say, but *how* you say it—your style. When you write an essay or article, book review or biography, you are writing for the eyes. When you write a speech, you are writing for the ear. It is possible that no one but you will ever see the words on the page; instead, listeners will hear your words as they travel through the air. For this reason, speeches require a completely different writing style from most other written works. You want to write much like you talk (although a very formal speech, such as an address by a president, is often written in a loftier style).

Pick up a book or magazine and turn to a random page. Now start reading out loud. How does it sound? Unless what you've grabbed happens to be written in a very conversational style, it probably sounds a bit stiff and formal—and not like anything you'd ever say in real life. That's because it was written to be read. And when we write things to be read, we usually try to follow the rules of grammar . We avoid sentence fragments and run-on sentences and perhaps try not to use contractions (such as "didn't" or "can't"). But listen to anyone talk for even a short time, and you will hear that his or her speech is littered with fragments, run-ons, and contractions, and it's fine if these "rule-breakers" appear in a speech as well (although you certainly still want to make sense and be intelligible).

Because your audience has no way to rewind what you have said and listen to it again, you want to keep your word choices as simple as possible. Remember, too, that you will eventually have to *speak* your speech and that long words might trip you up as you talk. In general, keep your sentences fairly short—both so that your audience can follow them and so that you can say them without having to pause for breath in awkward spots.

This doesn't mean that all of your sentences should be the same length, though. If they were, your speech would soon become monotonous, and some of your listeners might start drifting into daydreams. Varying your sentence length helps to create rhythm in your speech—and rhythm helps to create interest. To convey excitement, use short, urgent sentences. When you want to appear more relaxed, you can lengthen your sentences a bit, adding a pause here and there for emphasis.

Repetition and parallelism (in which two or more words follow the same pattern) can also help to create rhythm. Note the rhythm in the parallel phrases "of the people, by the people, for the people," for example.

The excerpt that follows is from a speech given by American lecturer Russell Conwell to a number of audiences across the U.S. (including one in Philadelphia) throughout the early 20th century. Read the excerpt out loud, and pay special attention to how it sounds.

U.S. president Abraham Lincoln delivering his famous Gettysburg Address (1863)

I would like to meet the great men who are here tonight. The great men! We don't have any great men in Philadelphia. Great men!...

Just as many great men here as are to be found anywhere. The greatest error in judging great men is that we think that they always hold an office....

I remember an incident that will illustrate this.... I am ashamed of it, but I don't dare leave it out. I close my eyes now; I look back through the years to 1863; I can see my native town....

The people had turned out to receive a company of soldiers, and that company came marching up on the Common.... I was but a boy, but I was captain of that company, puffed out with pride on that day....

[The mayor] thought that an office was all he needed to be a truly great man.... Suddenly his eyes fell upon me, and then the good old man came right forward and invited me to come up on the stand with the town officers. Invited me up on the stand!...

So I was invited up on the stand with the town officers. I took my seat and let my sword fall on the floor, and folded my arms across my breast and waited to be received. Napoleon the Fifth!...

[The mayor] had never made a speech in his life before, but he fell into the same error that others have fallen into; he seemed to think that the office would make him an orator. So he had written out a speech and walked up and down the pasture until he had learned it by heart and frightened the cattle, and he brought that manuscript with him, and, taking it from his pocket, he spread it carefully upon the table....

As you read, did you find this speech fairly easy to say out loud? That's because it was written for the ear rather than the eye. Notice how Conwell breaks the rules of grammar, with sentence fragments such as "The great men!" and "Napoleon the Fifth!" Short sentences help to drive the speech forward, while occasional longer sentences add variety and keep the speech from becoming monotonous. Conwell does not strive to sound educated or pretentious but instead relies on simple, informal words and phrases, speaking as if he were talking to a friend on the street. His informality helps to keep our interest, as does the humorous `tone` he has taken toward his subject.

And keeping the audience's interest is the number-one job of a speech. Without it, you might as well be talking to an empty room. But when subject and content, structure and style merge to capture an audience's attention, your message can get through—it can make people laugh, move them to tears, teach them a new skill, or even convince them to change their lives. So sit down and think about what your audience needs to know. Then turn it into a speech that's just waiting to be heard!

From Eye to Ear

It can take some practice to get used to writing for the ear rather than the eye. In order to focus on just the sound of a speech, it can help to turn a written piece into one that is ready to be spoken. First, find an article or essay that you find interesting and read it out loud. It will probably sound somewhat stiff, like it was written for the eye (which it was) rather than for the ear. Now try to rewrite it in a style that will sound good to the ear. As you work, aim to use short words and create a conversational tone. Don't be afraid to use sentence fragments and contractions. Pay attention to the rhythm of your words, too. When you are done, read your rewritten piece out loud. Does it sound like it was written for the ear?

A Solid Structure

Without a solid structure, your speech is likely to lose listeners. Practice building one with a speech about something you know how to do well, such as throwing a baseball. Before launching into your explanation, you need to get our attention, perhaps with a humorous anecdote, a startling statistic, or a colorful quote. Make sure your introduction also tells us why the information you are about to give us is important. In the body of your speech, tell us how to do whatever it is that you know how to do. Be sure to use `transitions` to lead from one point to the next so that we can keep up. Finish your speech with a powerful or humorous conclusion that will leave a lasting impression. After you have written your speech, deliver it to your family or friends. If they have trouble following along, `revise` your speech to make it clearer.

Powerful Persuasion

Think about something that you'd really like
to convince your parents to let you do or have.
Perhaps you'd like them to buy you an iPod, for
example. But how can you persuade them? Are they
likely to be moved by statistics about the popu-
larity of the iPod or a description of what it
does? Would an appeal to their reason or their
emotions—or both—be more effective? After you've
thought about the type of support that would be
most likely to help you win your case, try it!
Prepare a short speech that makes clear what it is
you're asking for and why you think you should have
it. Then give the speech to your parents. If they
say yes to your request, you've figured out how
to persuade them—at least in this case. But even
if they say no, you've had valuable practice in
developing support for an argument!

Paying Tribute

At some point in their lives, many people are called upon to given an occasional speech—a toast at a wedding, a eulogy at a funeral, or a tribute at an award ceremony, for example. Here's your chance! Imagine that your best friend is receiving an award (you decide for what), and you have been chosen to present it. You've been asked to give a short tribute to your friend. What will you say? Remember, you do not need to write a biography of your friend—just give us an overview of what makes him or her unique and why he or she is worthy of this honor. You can also incorporate an anecdote or two as you write out your speech. Keep things lighthearted (unless the award is for something very serious), and don't be afraid to inject some humor if appropriate.

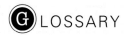LOSSARY

anecdotes brief stories recounting specific incidents or events

chronological following the order of time; something that is related chronologically tells what happened first, then what happened next, and so on

credibility the quality of inspiring belief; a credible speaker is one listeners trust as reliable

fiction literary works in which situations, characters, and events are made up; novels and short stories are works of fiction

grammar the rules that govern language and the correct formation of sentences

monotonous repetitious and unvaried

narration the telling of a story, as opposed to exposition (which generally provides background information)

nonfiction writing that is based on facts rather than fiction

prejudice a preformed, unfavorable opinion of someone or something founded on incomplete information or unreasonable feelings

Renaissance the time in European history, from the 14th through 16th centuries, that was marked by a renewal of classical art and literature and the beginnings of modern science and exploration

revise to rewrite for the purpose of improving

rhetoric the practice or study of using language effectively, especially in persuasive speaking

sound bites short statements, often taken from a longer speech, that are broadcast over the radio or television, usually as part of a news program

suffragist a person who works to extend suffrage, or voting rights, to people, especially women, who do not have them

tone the attitude of an author toward his or her subject

transitions words, phrases, or passages that connect one idea or section to another; "also," "in addition," and "on the other hand" are all examples of transitions

SELECTED (B)IBLIOGRAPHY

Carnegie, Dale, and Joseph Berg Esenwein. *The Art of Public Speaking*. New York: Cosimo Classics, 2007.

Copeland, Lewis, Lawrence W. Lamm, and Stephen J. McKenna, eds. *The World's Great Speeches*. Mineola, N.Y.: Dover Publications, 1999.

Ehrlich, Henry. *Writing Effective Speeches: The Ultimate Guide to Making Every Word Count*. New York: Reed Business Press, 2004.

Koch, Arthur. *Speaking with a Purpose*. Boston: Pearson Education, 2004.

Noonan, Peggy. *Simply Speaking: How to Communicate Your Ideas with Style, Substance, and Clarity*. New York: ReganBooks, 1998.

Safire, William, comp. *Lend Me Your Ears: Great Speeches in History*. New York: W.W. Norton & Company, 2004.

INDEX

LIGHTHOUSES
OF THE WORLD
A History of Where Land Meets Sea

Photography:

AGA Picture Library; pages 48-49, 61, 64, 65, 68,
69, 70, 75, 76, 78, 81, 118, 119.
Bildarkivet!/Ellbergs Bilder AB; cover, pages 158,
179, 180.
Robert V. Drapala; cover, page 184.
John Eagle; pages 138, 139, 140, 141, 142-143.
Johan Ebefors: page 160
Bengt Ekeholt/Bildbyrån i Göteborg AB; pages 162,
163, 183.
Magnus Enquist; cover, pages 144-145, 148, 155,
173, 175.
ET Archive, London; page 22.
Kurt Eriksson; page 89.
The Illustrated London News; pages 108, 109,
110-111, 112, 113, 114-115, 127.
Jens Karlsson/Bildbyrån i Göteborg AB; pages 160-161.
Wolfgang Kurz/INA Agency Press; page 169.
Sem Larsen/Bildbyrån i Göteborg AB; page 159
Terje Rakke; pages 156, 157.
Sven Rosenhall/GreatShots; page 149.
Claes-G Svanteson/Bildbyrån i Göteborg AB; page
159 (insert).
The Swedish National Art Museums; pages 106-107.
Jeppe Wikström/Pressens Bild; cover, pages 164, 166.
Anders Wästfelt; endpapers, pages 8-9, 24-25.
Sten Zackrisson; pages 116-117, 158 (insert),
161 (insert).

Lighthouses of The World has been originated and produced by
Nordbok International, Gothenburg, Sweden.

Editorial chief:
Göran Cederberg

Design, setting & photowork:
Designia, Munir Lotia

Illustrations:
Ulf Söderqvist together with Anders Engström

Authors:
Göran Cederberg, *chapter 1*
Ebbe Almqvist, *chapter 2,3*
Dan Thunman, *chapter 4,5*
Esbjörn Hillberg, *chapter 6*

Nordbok would like to express sincere thanks to all persons,
specially Esbjörn Hillberg, who have contributed in different
ways to the production of this book.

World copyright © 1999
Nordbok International,
P.O. Box 7095, SE-402 32 Gothenburg, Sweden

First published in the USA in 1999 by
CHARTWELL BOOKS, INC.
A Division of **BOOK SALES, INC.**
114 Northfield Avenue
Edison, New Jersey 08837

ISBN: 0-7858-1102-8

Printed in Portugal 1999

LIGHTHOUSES
OF THE WORLD
A History of Where Land Meets Sea

CHARTWELL
BOOKS, INC.

Contents

The History of Seafaring

N early three-fourths of the earth's surface is water. Almost all of it is sea water and ice, only about four percent being fresh water. The availability of pure fresh water has always been essential for our existence, so it is natural that water has been of basic importance for mankind through the ages. Moreover, water contains fish, crustaceans and other food that we have learned for thousands of years to catch, cultivate and exploit.

The boundary region between land and water has played a central role in human progress. Since prehistoric times, people have tried in different ways to make use of water and its possibilities, as when looking for better fishing areas and transporting goods by sea. The desire and need to dominate water – and the ability to overcome the dangers associated with gigantic masses of water – have enormously stimulated the improvement of ships as well as of aids to navigation. The farther from land we have moved with vessels, the more crucial it has become to know how to orient ourselves in relation to land. Thus, not only have boats been refined – from the first primitive, hollowed-out logs to today's huge, technically advanced ships – but also their instruments and methods of calculating positions, distances and directions.

Boats in ancient civilizations

Seafarers existed long before farmers. Already in the hunting and gathering stages of human life, people discovered how to build simple boats and floats for travel along rivers and coasts. Waterways had a great influence on the rise of early societies. Thanks to their rivers, people could reach remote territories and convey both settlers and goods to places that were difficult or impossible to reach by land. By using the water as a line of communication, cultures could expand farther.

The oldest boats we can certainly recognize were portrayed in Mesopotamia more than 5,000 years ago. Typical of these vessels were their straight sides – probably built with bundles of reeds tied together – and their high, somewhat curved prows.

Egyptian boats developed around the same time, but looked different. Representations on pottery show that their hulls were low, pointed, and curved slightly upward from the waterline. Apparently, they had driving paddles in the prow and steering oars at the stern, as well as a couple of deck cabins placed amidships. Shown on the cabins were poles that must have supported some kind of banner for identification of the vessels.

The large rivers which had boat traffic at a very early date are best exemplified by the Euphrates and Tigris in Mesopotamia, and by the Nile in Egypt. Presumably the cradle of modern seafaring lay in these regions, and the craft of sailing was later spread westward through the Mediterranean, by way of what are now Greece and Italy.

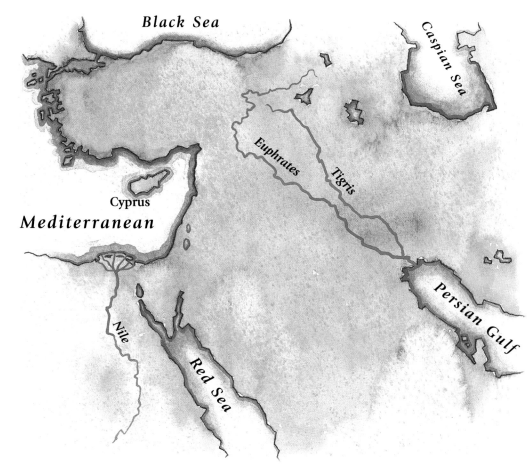

Black Sea

Caspian Sea

Euphrates

Tigris

Cyprus

Mediterranean

Nile

Red Sea

Persian Gulf

At Saqqara on the Nile, stone reliefs depicted improvements in ship-building until about 2500 B.C. The upper illustration here, from the tomb of Abibi, shows a so-called bipod mast, which had legs on each side of the midship line, so that its weight could be borne by the relatively weak hull. In addition, forestays and stern stays were used to strengthen the construction.

This illustration on left shows a relief from the tomb of Ipi at the same site, demonstrating more clearly how the boats were built.

In Northern Europe, ships were also built during the Bronze Age. They were framed canoes, probably covered with animal hides, or made in the clinker technique with broad thin planks and sewn together with rope. Illustrated here is a contemporary Scandinavian ship from a rock-carving.

In the Aegean Sea, migration and trade had long been employing boats, not least to obtain metals such as silver and copper. The smaller islands, then Crete, and finally the Greek mainland became centres of intense seafaring, which ranged as far as the coasts of the Near East and to parts of the Western Mediterranean. Already in the Early Bronze Age, pictures show long ships with high stems and many oars, besides characteristic fish-images and tassels on the prow.

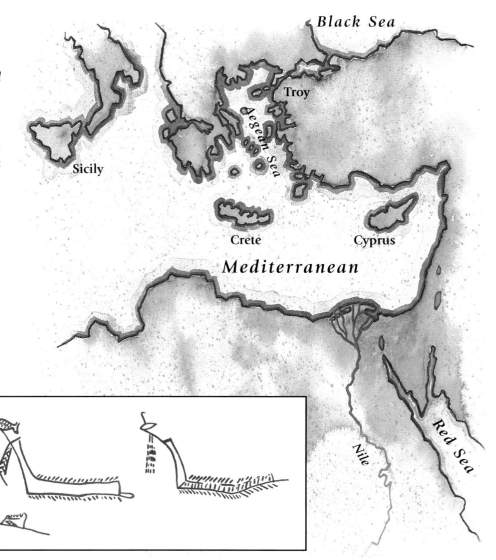

By 2000 B.C. there was an elaborate system of irrigation canals in Mesopotamia. The information recorded on clay tablets included maps giving the names of canals. These, and the rivers, were used to transport cattle, fish, grain, vegetables, stone and bricks. Hence, the system served both to interconnect the cities and to water the fields. In the illustration is a tablet from the city of Nippur, dated to about 1500 B.C., with canals named in cuneiform writing.

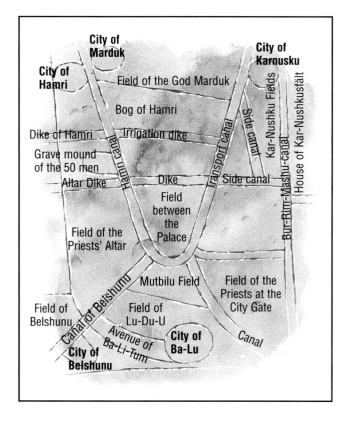

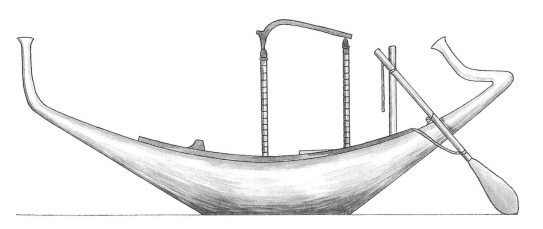

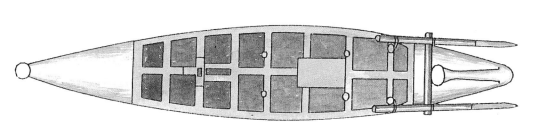

Detailed models of Nile boats have been found, for example, in the tomb of Meket-re at Thebes from about 2000 B.C. These models allow us to understand rather exactly how such vessels looked at the time. Here is the "banana-like" shape that remained typical for millennia on the river. Equally evident is the relationship to the older papyrus boats. A total length of 12-15 metres has been calculated for the actual vessels.

Harbours, too, became bigger. Great numbers of ships could now berth simultaneously for loading of goods. The commerce at seaports involved livestock, wine, oil, metals, precious stones, textiles and much else, not to mention slaves. With their merchant activity and good communications, these places soon turned into focal points of civilization. An illustration shows the lively scene in an Egyptian harbour about 1300 B.C.

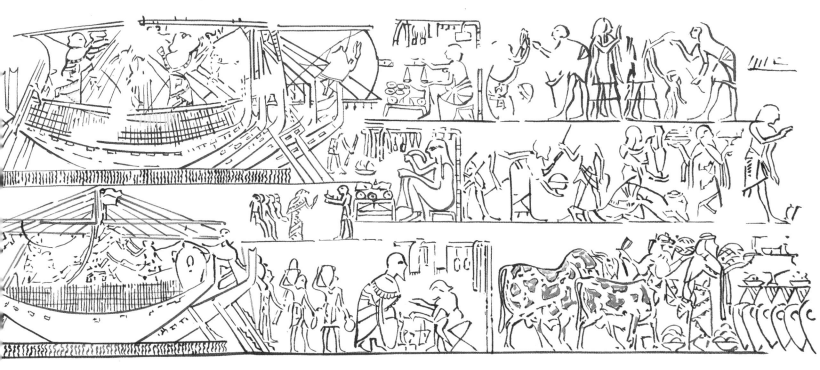

Developments in the Iron Age

Around 1000 B.C. a new sea power arose, the Phoenicians based on the coasts of Lebanon. For centuries, this area had been producing larger, more durable boats than the Egyptian ones. Strengthened by the use of cedar wood and by planking at both ends, they relied mainly on sails. Like other ancient seafarers, the Phoenicians normally did not sail out of sight of land, although rain and fog could render it invisible and call for good navigation even near shores. Neither were methods of sailing very sophisticated, and ships tended to follow the prevailing winds, which varied with the seasons. Still, Phoenicians became the leading traders in the Mediterranean and established many colonies, doing business as distantly as Cornwall in England. A result was that they learned more about sailing, and especially navigation, than their predecessors. Navigation by the stars, drawing on better astronomical knowledge, was doubtless their most systematic tool.

Greek seafaring, and that of the Etruscans in Italy, also grew rapidly at this time. Marine communication was encouraged not only by trade but by military and diplomatic needs, and it was much easier to transport people and goods by water than across rough country.

Anchors designed for boats in harbour had been used throughout the Bronze Age in the Eastern Mediterranean. At first they were only simple weights such as stones, but their forms did not change much in later periods. Illustrated on an Attic vase from about 440 B.C. is an anchor being cast into the water, while an oarsman manoeuvres the boat. Below is another such scene with a stock anchor. The stock was probably made of an extra-strong material, and the rest of ordinary wood.

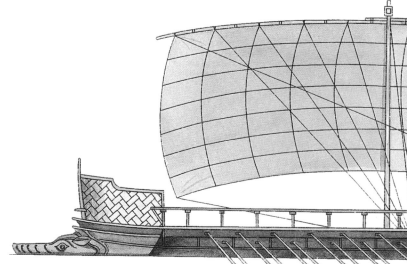

The first representation of a definitely seago-ing ship is dated to about 700 B.C. This relief, found in the ruins of Sanherib's palace in Assyria, showed a Phoenician vessel with sails and two rows of oars. It was probably a warship, since it had a ram at the prow – which enabled it to pen-etrate the hull of an enemy boat, then free itself without the hull tak-ing in water. Its flat upper deck, surrounded by shields, provid-ed a platform for the sol-diers to fight from.

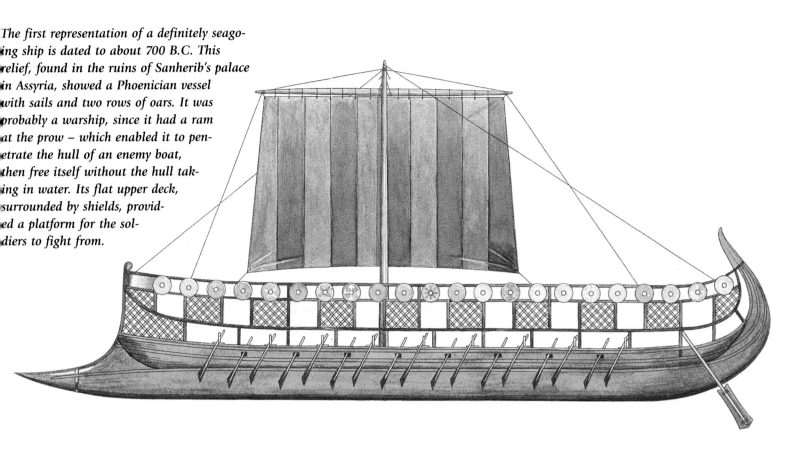

As the Greeks improved their merchant and naval fleets, finer ships were accompanied by more practical facilities in ports. Harbours and quays gained in both quantity and quality as bases for commerce. To regulate seafaring in the Mediterranean, a collection of maritime laws was introduced – the Lex Rhodia, named for the main city on the island of Rhodes. With its insistence on rights and obligations of sailors, it was a pioneer-ing attempt to govern working conditions in life at sea.

Aphrodisias
marble

Cyprus

Rhodes

Mediterranean

Alexandria

Nile

The Romans go to sea

The Roman Empire's expansion around the time of Christ brought a vast transformation to the region's waters. Initially, the Romans had no tradition of seafaring, and no fleet of their own. But they learned quickly and, within a few generations, the entire Mediterranean was more or less a Roman sea. Comprehensive commerce went on, and goods from the whole known world – including spices from India – could be bought in the streets of Rome. Some have said that this marine dominance can only be compared to what the British achieved during the early nineteenth century.

Since there were no compasses, all navigation in the dark was done by the stars. It was also essential for a skipper to learn how the winds and currents behaved according to the hour and month. Special descriptions for sailing were written, with instructions and information about bearings, distances in sailing days, and so on. Such pilot-books or "portolans" were in use by A.D. 100.

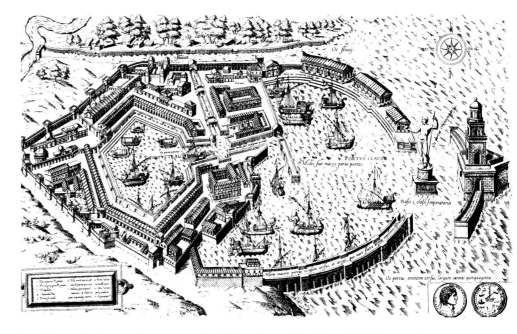

In order to berth ever larger vessels, old harbours like that of Ostia near Rome were improved. Around the year 200, Ostia was a seething port with a rich commercial life. It had a considerable population, and most of the features that characterized subsequent ports – from stores and workshops to bars and bordellos. Diverse handicrafts were practised, mainly connected with the busy seagoing trade.

Shipbuilders were refining their own resources, and the boats increasingly resembled those of today. Prominent was the clinker-built hull, in which the frame was added afterward. The illustration here, however, is of a trading ship in the carvel technique – without overlapping planks – using two sails and double steering oars. It is a reconstruction from a relief in the harbour of Ostia.

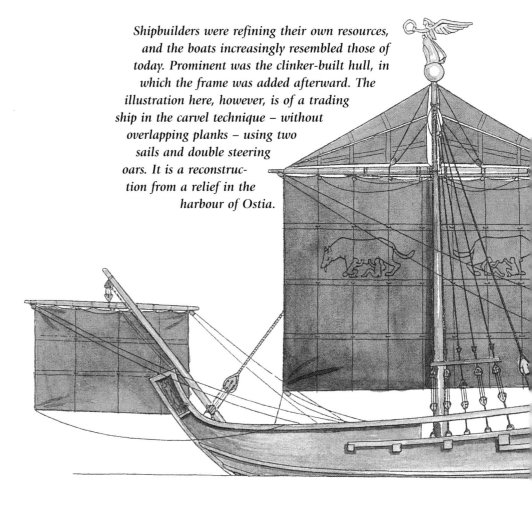

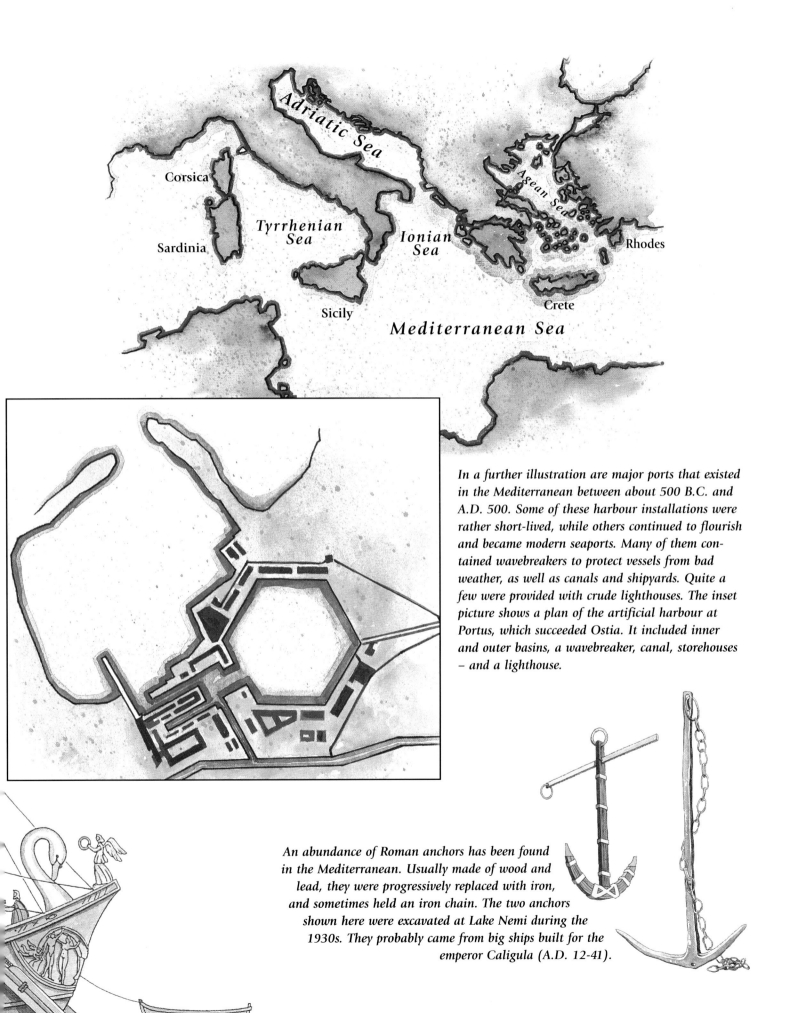

In a further illustration are major ports that existed in the Mediterranean between about 500 B.C. and A.D. 500. Some of these harbour installations were rather short-lived, while others continued to flourish and became modern seaports. Many of them contained wavebreakers to protect vessels from bad weather, as well as canals and shipyards. Quite a few were provided with crude lighthouses. The inset picture shows a plan of the artificial harbour at Portus, which succeeded Ostia. It included inner and outer basins, a wavebreaker, canal, storehouses – and a lighthouse.

An abundance of Roman anchors has been found in the Mediterranean. Usually made of wood and lead, they were progressively replaced with iron, and sometimes held an iron chain. The two anchors shown here were excavated at Lake Nemi during the 1930s. They probably came from big ships built for the emperor Caligula (A.D. 12-41).

The Vikings – warriors and traders

In the far north, the Viking Age has been veiled by myths and legends. The "furious Norsemen" did much harm, for instance in the British Isles. Yet their fame rested chiefly on skill as seafarers. They had a solid tradition of shipbuilding and had learned to construct vessels that were well suited to their needs.

The oldest finds of Scandinavian boats date from about 350 B.C., and the next oldest from A.D. 350-400. Sails are still lacking, so

apparently there was no knowledge of how to use the wind for power. Already the typical shapes of Viking ships are suggested, but these do not emerge clearly until some centuries later. By 700, the Vikings were becoming adept at sailing, and a hundred years afterward they began to leave their coastal waters for regular raids and explorations.

With this combination of advantages for commerce and battle, Viking vessels spread wonder and terror in many parts of Europe. Full of warriors, equipment and horses, they could lay the long side parallel to a beach and be emptied with amazing speed.

A Viking ship was broad and flat-bottomed, which made it shallow-going and easy to land on beaches, or to pull overland at difficult rapids in rivers. It could also be heavily loaded, and was thus both an excellent trading vessel and a superb warship, ideal for surprise attacks. Despite their basically similar structure, the traders were somewhat shorter and wider than the "long ships" used mostly for fighting.

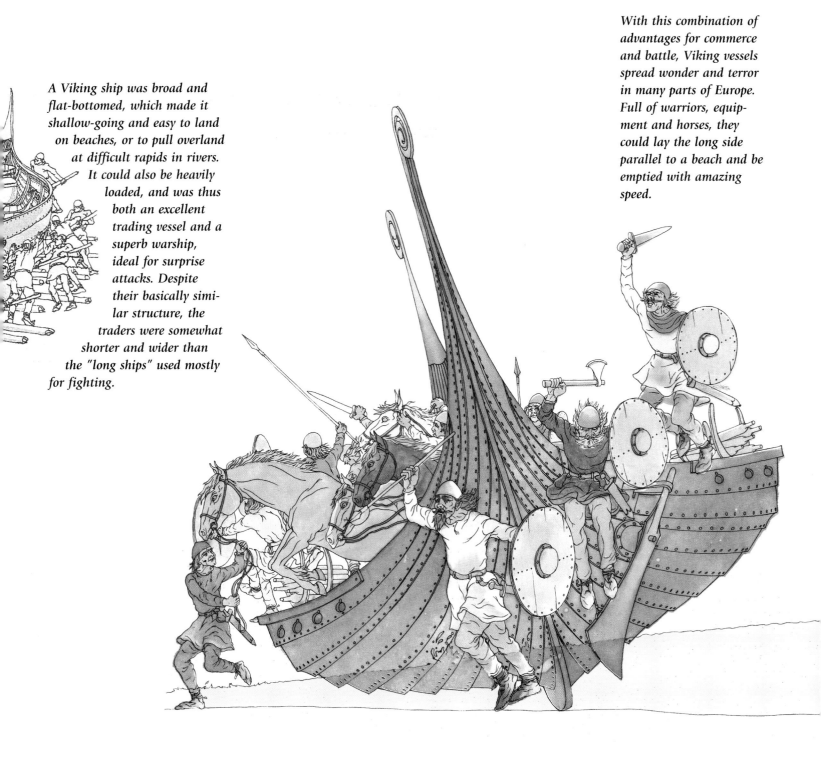

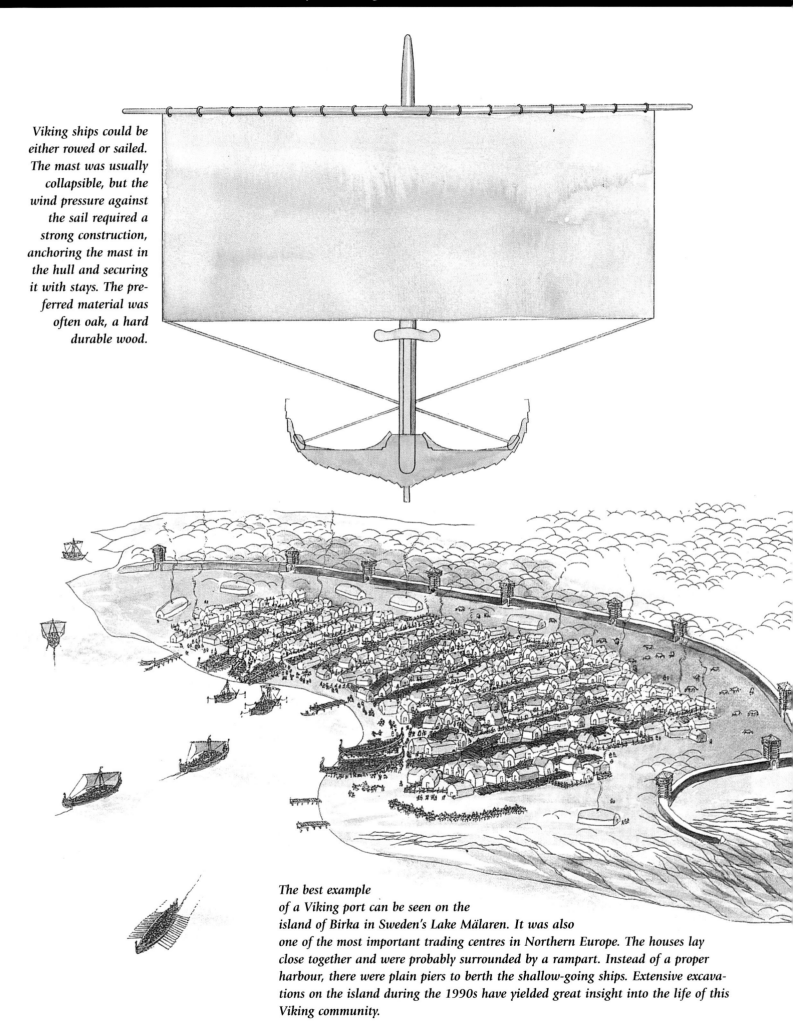

Viking ships could be either rowed or sailed. The mast was usually collapsible, but the wind pressure against the sail required a strong construction, anchoring the mast in the hull and securing it with stays. The preferred material was often oak, a hard durable wood.

The best example of a Viking port can be seen on the island of Birka in Sweden's Lake Mälaren. It was also one of the most important trading centres in Northern Europe. The houses lay close together and were probably surrounded by a rampart. Instead of a proper harbour, there were plain piers to berth the shallow-going ships. Extensive excavations on the island during the 1990s have yielded great insight into the life of this Viking community.

Greenland

Iceland

Birka

Kaupang

North Sea

Hamburg

Dorestad

Paris

Bordeaux

Rome

Lisbon

Sicily

Kiev

Caspian Sea

Black Sea

Jerusalem

Crete

Mediterranean

Alexandria

The customary claim that Christopher Columbus discovered the New World has recently been revised. Literature and archaeology agree that the first Europeans who set foot on that continent were Vikings. Around the year 1000, Leif Eriksson sailed via Iceland and southern Greenland to reach "Vinland" in northeastern North America, and returned to tell the tale.

The Vikings faced the problem of ocean sailing for days, even weeks, out of sight of land. They had to become clever navigators, and must have depended primarily on observing the stars. It is believed that they also used a simple kind of compass, of which a reconstruction is shown here.

New ships and new opportunities

During the later Middle Ages, a more advanced type of vessel was launched - the cog. These ships had a streamlined hull with concave lines. They were rapid and robust, with fine sailing characteristics. A distinguishing feature was the lookout post, up on the mast. Just as important was their high freeboard, almost invulnerable to attack by long ships and other rowed war vessels in the North Sea and the Baltic. From the lofty deck, archers with crossbows could easily repulse an enemy. In the fifteenth century, cogs changed their appearance by adding another mast or two, at the fore and stern.

Shipbuilding and navigation benefitted from the longer voyages to remote regions. As vessels grew larger and safer, people lost their fear of crossing oceans. There was also an increasing awareness that the earth was round, not flat. One of the most famous expeditions was certainly that of Columbus, who on August 3, 1492, left the harbour of Palos in his ship Santa Maria to find a westward route to India. As we know, he did not get there but "discovered" America. Illustrated here is a reconstruction of the Santa Maria, with an inset picture of Columbus.

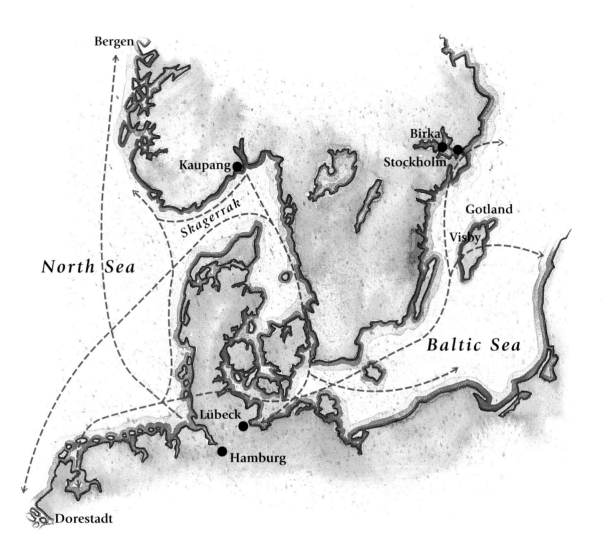

During the so called "Hansa period" of lively merchant traffic in northern Europe. Food and other necessities were freighted continually between cities. The trade routes were much the same as in Viking times, but the faster and stabler ships were even less limited to coastal travel. Besides Lübeck and Hamburg in northern Germany, Bergen and Visby were among the leading Hansa ports.

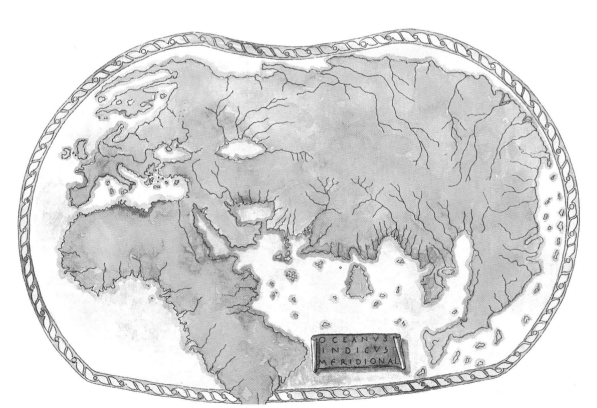

By the end of the fifteenth century, geographers had a fairly good view of how the world looked. This map from 1497 was painted by Martellus Germanus. America is missing but Europe, Asia and Africa are represented with surprising accuracy.

Exploring the seas

Long-distance voyages became common during the sixteenth century. The first trip around the world was made in 1519. Europeans landed in many exotic places, often conquering and plundering. Colonies were founded and trade prospered. Spices, silk, porcelain, costly metals and other rare items were taken back to Europe, where harbours expanded as never before. Both warships and merchant vessels developed further, and several countries started "East India Companies" to trade with goods from China and other distant lands.

Supply ports were established along the sea routes, and geographical knowledge improved. With the period of the great clipper ships, virtually all the main routes would become familiar and blank spots on the world map filled with traffic. Navigation was ever more reliable, and scientific passengers such as Darwin were to follow, making revolutionary discoveries about natural and human life.

As technology and curiosity progressed, remarkable expeditions were undertaken. The voyages of Captain James Cook are a good example. He sailed around New Zealand, landed in Australia, visited numerous other islands and, in 1772, tried to find the "southern continent" at the South Pole. Although he never got there, he came within 1,300 nautical miles of it, the closest any human being had been to this inhospitable part of the planet.

During the 1700s seafaring flourished in most parts of Europe. New harbours sprang up and the old ones grew – but to satisfy the increasing demands on the merchant fleets, their ships also had to be made larger, faster and safer. The same trends, and others in political life, led to ever more powerful military vessels. This painting from the 1780s shows the bustling shipyard of the Swedish royal navy at Karlskrona.

Not only did explorers and famous seamen dare to
enter unknown waters. Hunters of the big game in the
oceans, too, were seeking new territory. A specially
built whaling ship in action is illustrated
here, with its undersails furled and a lookout
on the mast. Also shown are some of the
harpoons and other equipment used
by whalers.

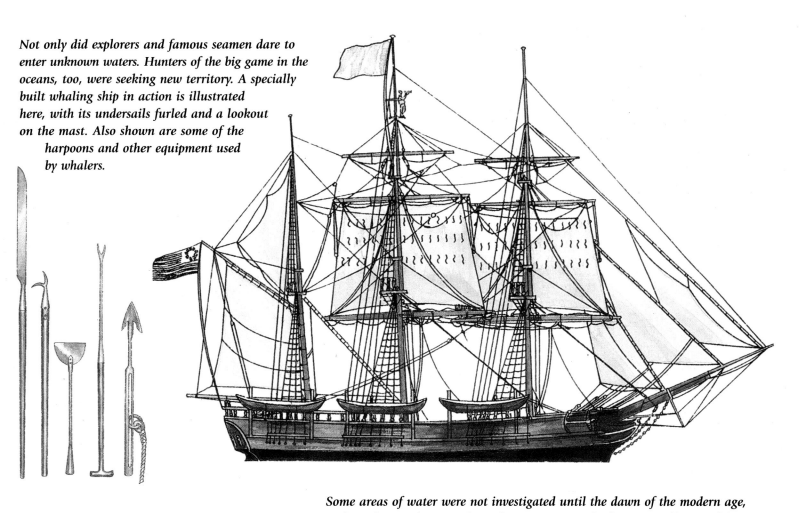

Some areas of water were not investigated until the dawn of the modern age,
such as the Northwest and Northeast Passages. The latter was discovered in
1878-79 by the Swedish explorer Adolf Erik
Nordenskiöld, who sailed along the north
coast of Siberia and down through the
Bering Strait into the Pacific.

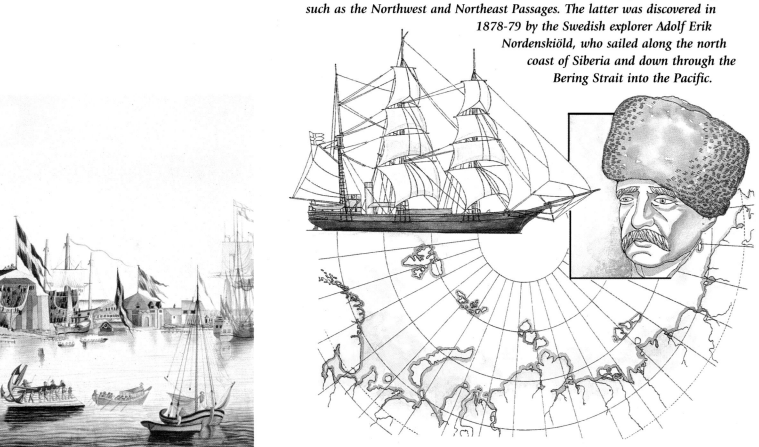

Th[e]
the Li[ght]

For ages, the seaways have been p[...]
nication. When merchant seafaring [...]
ships tended to sail by day and near coasts. [...]
home shores, one learned to observe and record
the coast and, for example, islands, headlands, cove[s]
teristic details such as mountains, stone blocks and trees,
could serve as landmarks on the return voyage.

The natural landmarks soon proved insufficient, so sailors
built easily recognizable towers and cairns, or built on special
natural landmarks to make them more prominent. Later, coastal
navigation was made easier by sailing descriptions, called periploi,
which gave the routes between various harbours and were extended by generations of sailors. These descriptions also showed
the directions of winds and ocean currents under normal conditions. There were also primitive maps and simple harbour
charts, known as portolans. The oldest periplus that has been
preserved, from the sixth century A.D., is attributed to Skylax
of Caryanda. It contains information on routes and, among
other things, shoals and water depths, anchoring sites, currents
and harbour entrances. The water depth was measured with a
lead line, and contemporary anchors consisted of a weight tied
on a rope.

The lighthouse's origins

As long as people have sailed at sea, the sight of fire has warned them of danger. Homer's Odyssey (700 B.C.) mentions the use of fires and flares to guide sailors and for signalling. It was a long step forward from there to maintaining permanent fires for sailing at night. But ever since the first bonfires were lit, there has been a constant effort to improve the beacon's power so that it can be seen at greater distances.

The first beacons recorded in writing were built by the Greeks in the fifth and sixth centuries B.C., primarily to mark the entrances of harbours, such as Piraeus. On the other hand, not a single beacon is mentioned in the contemporary sailing directions, which covered all the Mediterranean coasts.

The oldest known "beacons" were fairway fires on shores. Their light was not very strong, and they had to be tended continually. Moreover, fixed beacons were often confused with other lights on land. Another serious disadvantage was that no sailor could be certain where the fires were located or when they were lit. It even happened that false beacons were lit to run ships aground and plunder them.

Around 290 B.C. a harbour beacon named the Colossus was erected at the harbour entrance of Rhodes. Some 40 metres high, this bronze statue of the sun-god Helios had a fire on top. It was built by Chares of Lindos, and destroyed 80 years later by an earthquake.

*The most famous beacon of ancient times was
a structure, 130 metres high, on the isle of
Pharos at the entrance to the Egyptian harbour of Alexandria, the biggest port ever in the
Roman Empire. Built by Sostratos of Knidos
in 299-288 B.C., it served as a navigation
mark. From the first century A.D., a fire
was kept burning on a platform at its
top. According to seafarers then, the
fire was visible up to 40 km away.
In 1302, however, an earthquake
destroyed the building.*

Similar "fire-towers" were raised during the last centuries B.C., when Phoenicians, Egyptians and Romans began to voyage for trading and military purposes even by dark. The towers became landmarks at important harbours, for instance in the Aegean Sea (Piraeus, Smyrna), the Black Sea (Herakleia Pontica, Timeae), on the coasts of North Africa (Carthage) and southern Spain (Turris Caepionis, Gades) and in Sicily (Messina).

Under the emperor Claudius, around A.D. 50, the harbour of Ostia near Rome was built – with a beacon behind a huge statue of the emperor. Other harbours with beacons were at Ravenna (Classis, Pomposa) and Puteoli, built about 10 B.C. under the emperor Augustus; Centumcellae (A.D. 120) under Hadrian; and Leptis Magna (A.D. 200) under Septimus Severus.

Once the Roman Empire expanded, many beacons were built in Mediterranean harbours, as well as some on the Atlantic coasts of Spain and France, all the way up to the English Channel. Sometimes oil lamps were used for light in the small harbour beacons.

About A.D. 40, the emperor Caligula took his army through France to Dover on the south coast of England. Four years later a triumphal tower, the Tour d'Ordre, was built at Boulogne with a beacon on top, as a monument to the conquest of France. This tower also served for defence, and in 811 it was damaged by the Vikings, so badly that the emperor Charlemagne had to repair it at great cost. Finally in 1644 it fell into the sea. At Dover, too, a beacon tower was erected in memory of England's conquest around the same time.

In the city of Coruña at Spain's northwest corner, a beacon tower called the Torre de Hercules has stood since the first century A.D. and is actually still used. It was probably built to guide the Spanish merchant shipping to Ireland.

Early aids to navigation

As long as people sailed on rivers, they got home easily – but once they left land and made ever more advanced ocean voyages, the need for landmarks and navigational aids grew rapidly.

On the open sea, one must be able to figure out positions. Ancient sailors made use of the stars. Astronomy and geometry were familiar to the Greeks since around 500 B.C. and they used the movements of both the sun and stars to calculate positions. For example, it was known that the height of the Pole Star above the horizon varied with latitude. By measuring the angle between this star's rays and the vertical, one could estimate the latitude of one's position. These calculations, and an understanding of weather factors, enabled the long-distance voyagers of that age to find their way home. Also developed were crude, but working, instruments to determine position, water depth, speed and direction, but these were to be perfected only in the sixteenth century or later.

During the centuries, two navigational instruments were perfected that made use of star observations, the astrolabe and the cross-staff. Their principle was to calculate the position of the point of observation from two other points, whose mutual relationship was known. The astrolabe originated among the Babylonians. Masters of its manufacture were the Arabs, who had great knowledge in mathematics and astronomy. The planispheric astrolabe, reputedly developed by Hipparchus (150 B.C.) and Apollonius of Perga (240 B.C.), gave an exact, simple measuring instrument to seafarers.

The astrolabe and how it was used to find the elevations of heavenly bodies.

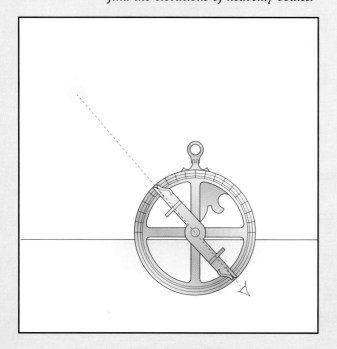

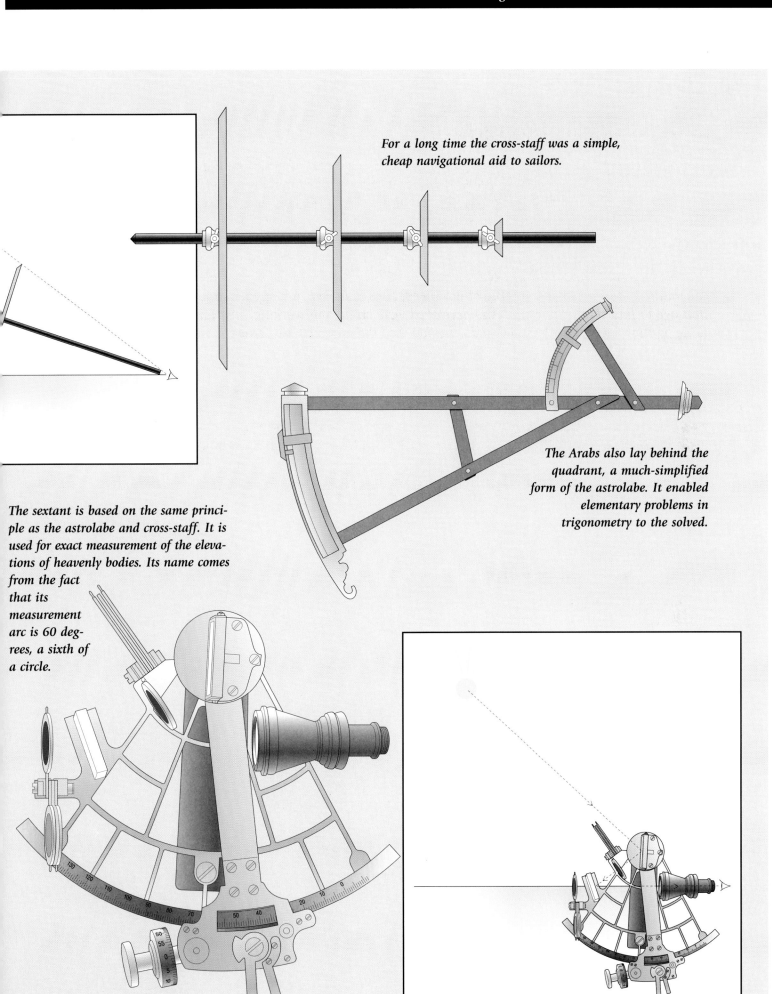

For a long time the cross-staff was a simple, cheap navigational aid to sailors.

The Arabs also lay behind the quadrant, a much-simplified form of the astrolabe. It enabled elementary problems in trigonometry to the solved.

The sextant is based on the same principle as the astrolabe and cross-staff. It is used for exact measurement of the elevations of heavenly bodies. Its name comes from the fact that its measurement arc is 60 degrees, a sixth of a circle.

The "Dark" Ages

Towards the end of Roman times, around A.D. 400, there were 30 beacons between the Black Sea and the Atlantic. But they were put out after the fall of the Empire, and stayed out until the early 1100s. Throughout this period, dominated by migrations and wars, no progress was made with lighthouses; new ones were not built and the old ones were partially destroyed. Merchant shipping decreased and, in the existing ports, only local trading was done. Their beacons were not lit, so that possible enemies would not be guided by them to attack.

The Frankish kingdom, formed in the sixth century, was in commercial contact with Scandinavia, but also in conflict with it. Now the northern Europeans also began venturing onto the seas. This led to much shipbuilding in Scandinavia, and Viking vessels predominated until the 1100s. When the Viking raids started in the late 700s, there were no unified realms in the far north. It was individual pirates who carried out the coastal raids and plunderings that shook Europe. The Franks were attacked by the Danish king Godfred in the early 800s, but only in the 900s were France and England struck by better-organized Danish forces under royal command. In 1066, however, the Viking raids stopped with the death of Harald Hårdråde.

Characteristic of the dragon-headed Viking ships, besides their shape, was that an oar steered them – not a rudder. This way of manoeuvring was physically very hard, and could not be used on any ship with a large displacement. Moreover, it was unknown how to beat to windward – sail against the wind – and oars had to be used for such movement.

At some places along the French and English coasts in the 800s, local beacons were managed by private interests – often churches and chapels. The beacon usually consisted of tallow or wax lights, shining from the building's windows. Monks and hermits settled on remote coasts and islands that were dangerous to sailors, warned them of dangers and saved those who were shipwrecked, eventually also salvaging lost cargo. In time, they received compensation, a fee proportional to the value of what was salvaged, and this increased the motivation for such philanthropic activities.

The opportunity of profiting by others' disasters led pirates to light false beacons and lure ships to be wrecked and plundered. False beacons are mentioned already about 700 B.C., and still occurred in the 1800s. But during the 1100s, Richard the Lionhearted introduced awful penalties for pirates who misguided seafarers.

Cordouan's history

In the 13th century, Spain had close commercial connections with the French port of Bordeaux in the bay of Gironde. There, French wines were traded for cordovan leather from the Moorish city of Cordova in southern Spain. At the Atlantic mouth of the bay of Gironde, many shipwrecks were caused by strong currents and shoals, so the authorities of Bordeaux built a primitive wood-fired beacon on a cliff, which was named Cordouan to honour their Spanish trading partners. The beacon was financed with fees paid by all passing ships to its keeper, a city employee. On this model, fee-supported beacons were soon built at many other ports. Trade-minded businessmen and opportunists took the chance to earn money by building their own private beacons. As a result, various governments later issued privileges that gave contracts to individuals for building light-houses.

The primitive beacon at the bay of Gironde was replaced in 1360 by a stone tower, 16 metres high, in memory of a victory over the French in 1356 by Prince Edward of Wales. In 1584, Louis de Foix built a magnificent tower 37 metres high on the Cordouan cliff – a project that took all of 26 years. During 1788-90, the tower was renovated by the architect Joseph TeulËre, who preserved only the chapel in the lower storey. The new tower was also heightened from 37 to 68 metres, and it is still used today.

Measuring instruments

Gauges of nautical speed, or rather distance, have a famous ancestor in Heron's hodometer. An early model was described already by Vitruvius around the time of Christ. It made use of the rotational speed of the blades in a little "mill" that was lowered into the water. An Italian, Leon Battista Alberti (1404-72), in his Ludi Matematici, describes another type of speedometer, which uses the wind strength to calculate the vessel's speed. This instrument, both complicated and unreliable, was later criticized heavily by Leonardo da Vinci.

Much more exact was the chip log, first described by an Englishman, William Bourne, in 1574. It consists of a wooden disc, forming the sector of a circle, and a lead weight that makes it float vertically with some water resistance. To the wood was fastened a log line, divided with knots into definite lengths (8 fathoms = 1 knot). By letting the line run out for a certain time, the speed could be found in knots, and thus in nautical miles per hour.

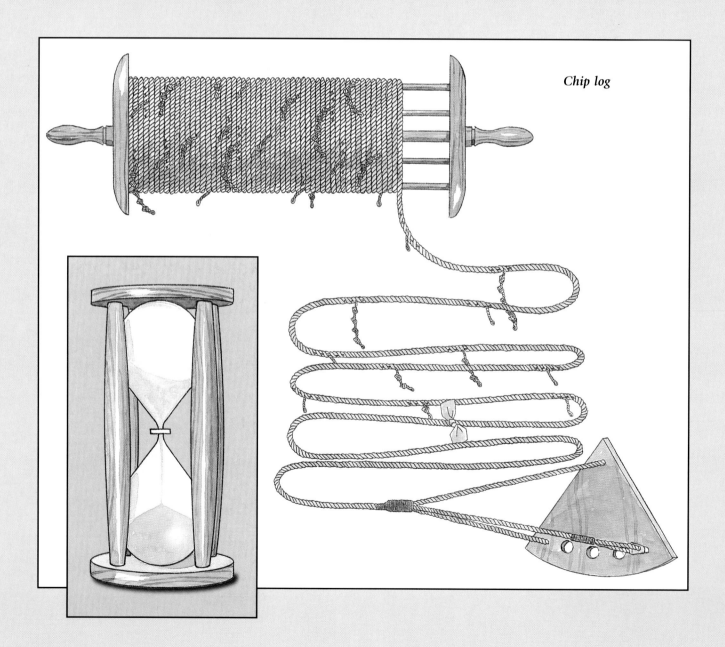

Chip log

The compass

During the eleventh century, the Chinese used a simple compass to orient themselves at sea. It was a magnetic needle stuck into a short cane tube, floating in a bowl of water. But this was impractical on a rolling ship. The Arabs knew of the compass before it reached Europe, where it was developed by an Italian, Flavio Gioja from Amalfi. Around 1250, Mediterranean sailors began using a disc that was divided into degrees (the compass rose) with a rotating needle suspended on a pin in its centre. Towards the end of that century, compasses acquired a gimbal mounting that kept the needle horizontal. In the 1800s, ships began to be built of steel, whose magnetism disturbed the compass. This influence had to be compensated by placing small magnetic rods near the compass.

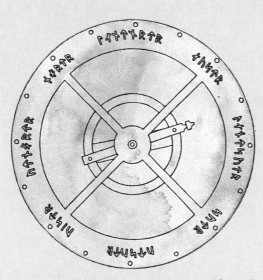

A reconstruction of a Scandinavian compass from the 1300s.

Compass from 1345.

Compass from 1545.

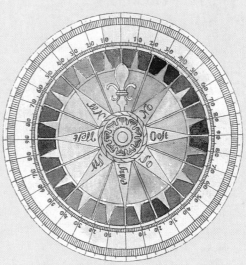

Compass from the end of the 1800s.

Seafaring starts again

When law and order were re-established in the 1100s, European merchant shipping commenced in two separate regions – the Mediterranean and along the coasts of the North and Baltic Seas. At new trading centres, beacons were built in river estuaries and harbour entrances.

The history of seafaring in southern Europe between 1050 and 1300 is dominated by the Crusades. Through voyages to the holy places in the eastern Mediterranean lands, new attractive markets and trading partners were found. Thus, profit soon became a stronger motive for these trips than religious faith. The new business opportunities that opened up were quickly discovered by the Italian maritime cities of Genoa, Venice and Pisa. They obtained commercial concessions and built harbours that gave them a monopoly on trade with the Orient, which also led to conflicts and wars.

In the mid-1100s, beacons were built in both Genoa and Meloria (near Livorno). The latter's is believed to have been the first beacon built on a rock in the sea. Around 1190, Messina in Sicily received a new beacon-tower, thanks to its strategic location as a junction, and its key role as a port and trading city during the Crusades. In other Mediterranean coastal cities, too, beacons were built as a result of the prospering merchant trade.

A lighthouse known as the Capo di Faro, nicknamed "Lanterna", was built at Genoa in 1543. With a height of 76 metres, it was the world's tallest – until 1902 when the French lighthouse at Ile Vierge, 83 metres high, was completed.

The Hansa League creates networks of lighthouse

Already in 1280, groups of German businessmen collaborated to protect their common interests. Consequently, they founded a league including Lübeck and other German trading cities. Formally dating from 1385, the Hansa League came to dominate the Baltic trade until the mid- 1500s. Linked to it were also foreign cities such as Bruges, London, Bergen, Visby, Riga and Novgorod. Through co-operation between these trading places, several lighthouses were built along the Scandinavian and German coasts during the 1200s, 1300s and 1400s.

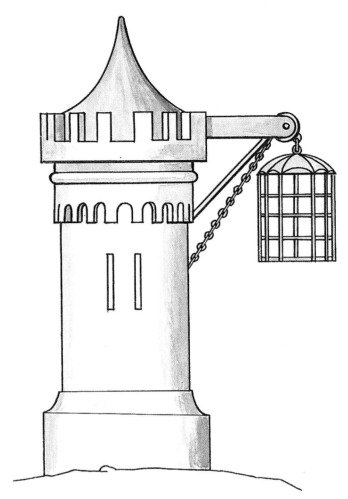

In the early 1200s, Lübeck was an imposing merchant port. Due to its wishes, King Valdemar II of Denmark erected a beacon on Cape Falsterbo, for the safety of seafaring through the Öresund strait. This was the first state-built beacon in northern Europe. It was followed, around 1225, by a harbour beacon which Lübeck built at Travemünde in Germany.

While no formal connections existed with the Italian maritime cities, the first regulations of the Hansa League used Venice as their model. They had the same goal: to create trading bases and monopolies as well as protecting merchant shipping by combating piracy, and decreasing the losses from capsizing and grounding. This was done by marking out fairways with beacons and buoys, and by training pilots. The trading places where Italian businessmen primarily met colleagues from the Hansa League were located in Flanders. There, sea-marks and beacons were set up during the 1200s and 1300s by local Dutch seamen and fishermen.

The struggle over merchant shipping

After some decades of protectionism, the Hansa League met stiff resistance, especially from Danes. The non-German countries on the Baltic created their own leagues, which decreased the Hansa's importance during the 1400s. At the same time, Italian maritime powers declined and Portugal took the lead as a seafaring nation. But conflicts with Spain over new colonies soon resulted in Spain, Holland, and to some extent England becoming the main European traders. In the mid-1500s, the Dutch controlled all freight traffic between the Baltic countries and points westward, while England was far behind in seafaring. This is also reflected in the marking of sea routes.

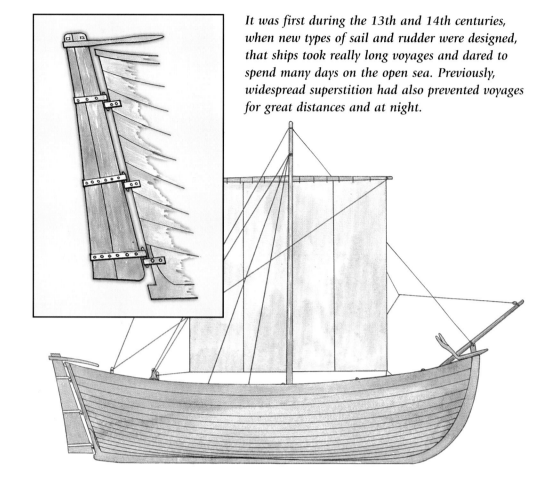

It was first during the 13th and 14th centuries, when new types of sail and rudder were designed, that ships took really long voyages and dared to spend many days on the open sea. Previously, widespread superstition had also prevented voyages for great distances and at night.

TRINITAS IN UNITATE

Before England's official maritime and pilotage administration, Trinity House, was founded in 1514, the country's coastal lighthouses were managed privately by church orders or charity funds. In the early 1600s, however, England could again compete with Holland for the leading role in seafaring. Due to these nations' competition, the Hansa league was finally dissolved. England, helped by protectionism (the Navigation Act of 1651), a strategic geographical location, and rapid technical progress, was able to gain supremacy over merchant shipping. In the 1600s and 1700s, English sea-marking expanded greatly. Most of the new beacons were privately built and owned by prominent people, who were entitled to take tolls from passing ships. But in 1836, Parliament decided that Trinity House would buy up the private beacons. Thus England, earlier than other nations, ensured a unified service for seafarers all round its coasts. Shown here is a map of the lighthouses that existed across Europe until the 1600s.

The techniques of classic beacons

Slow changes took place in the kinds of light source used. The early flares and open fires were replaced, during the first century A.D., by burning candles or simple oil lamps. The oil lamp, developed by the Egyptians, was also widely used by the Greeks and Romans. Wood fires were at first completely unprotected from the weather, but a roof and a landward wall were built later at some beacons. However, there were still problems with wood supply, the difficulty of maintaining a wood fire, and sometimes serious dimming of the light by smoke. Besides, fire could cause conflagrations during storms. Candles and oil lamps became a good alternative only when they could be enclosed in lanterns, as glass became available after the 1200s. Yet glass had poor transparency until the 1700s, and was hard to keep clean.

In 1561, coal was first used as a fuel at the lighthouse of Kullens, then in Denmark, which had a rocker light. From the 1600s until the 1700s, a well-kept open coal fire was considered the most effective light source, as it could be seen for at least 10-12 kilometres if the light was reflected by the clouds. During this period, attempts were begun to enclose coal fires with glass, and later to provide them with blast-air.

During the
1500s, when ships
were first manoeuvred into
harbours even at night, a leading
light was introduced at North Shields in
England. This meant a low tower and a high tower,
about 200 metres apart, with tallow lamps that shone in a narrow sector.
The seafarer's course was correct when the sources were vertically aligned. In the
1600s, several lamps were clustered at a place so that the beacon could be
recognized and distinguished from other lights on land.

Oil lamps consisted of a woollen-yarn wick on a reservoir made of stone, clay or metal, which was filled with some vegetable oil or fish oil. This type of lamp was very inefficient until 1782, when a Swiss scientist, Alme Argand, invented a lamp that was ten times brighter. The Argand lamp had a ring-shaped wick, which greatly increased the air draught and thus burned with a clearer flame. Only in the 1800s did lamp oil and lamp gas arrive. At the same time, mechanical aids were invented to make the lamp's light blink.

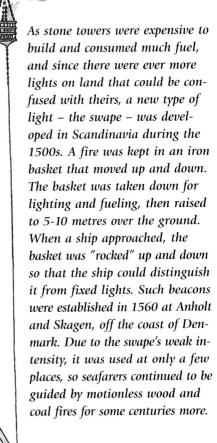

As stone towers were expensive to build and consumed much fuel, and since there were ever more lights on land that could be confused with theirs, a new type of light – the swape – was developed in Scandinavia during the 1500s. A fire was kept in an iron basket that moved up and down. The basket was taken down for lighting and fueling, then raised to 5-10 metres over the ground. When a ship approached, the basket was "rocked" up and down so that the ship could distinguish it from fixed lights. Such beacons were established in 1560 at Anholt and Skagen, off the coast of Denmark. Due to the swape's weak intensity, it was used at only a few places, so seafarers continued to be guided by motionless wood and coal fires for some centuries more.

Since tallow and wax lamps are point sources, they were very effective in combination with a reflector. Simple metal reflectors were adopted in the mid-1500s (Gollenberg, 1532). Where stronger sources were needed, candelabras with many lamps were used later.

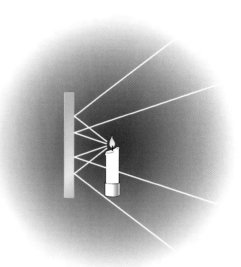

Ancient beacons were mainly stone towers where wood, charcoal, or tar on a cooker. The towers were cairns at first, but later were mortared and had an external or internal stairway for transport of the fuel. These lighthouses were often clumsy. In spite of this, similar towers were used until the 1800s at places where a strong light was needed. Some of the smaller lighthouses that were built by the Italian trading states, the Hansa League, church beacon-orders and private individuals, acquired ever more slender towers with candles and oil lamps in the 1400s and 1500s.

Lighthouse technology

During the 17th century, when the growth in seafaring increased the need for lighthouses, it began to be realized that traditional fire-beacons demanded too much work and wood, and should be replaced by directed light sources. This led to the technical development of coal beacons, as well as of light amplification and blinking lights in beacons with weaker light sources.

The new sources enabled lighthouse towers to be built of wood, but these did not resist storms as strongly as stone towers. Since ships were becoming larger and the traffic heavier, it proved necessary to built beacons also on rocks out at sea – and with their very hard weather conditions, new lighthouse structures were required. The innovations in building, which were to be used for a long time afterward in such conditions, came from an Englishman, John Smeaton (1724-92). In 1759 he erected a beacon of individually shaped, interlinked stone blocks on the famous Eddystone Rock near England's south coast. Smeaton was also the first to use reinforced concrete in construction, as he strengthened the beacon's walling with a mixture of mortar and iron pieces, which was a primitive kind of reinforced concrete. Moreover, this was the first use since Roman times of cement that hardens in water, which predominated for building lighthouses by the end of the 19th century.

Developments from 1600 until 1800

When wood and coal beacons became impractical, and lanterns grew common in lighthouses, candle and oil lamps were used ever more often. Both of these sources, however, had the disadvantage of producing much soot and smoke, which dimmed the light and blackened the lantern glass, calling for constant maintenance.

Not until the 1600s, therefore, did oil lamps see widespread use. Before the mid-1800s, when shale oil and petroleum went into production, raw or refined oils of animal or vegetable origin were burned – especially spermaceti oil and colza oil, which were both expensive. Next came cheaper, locally extracted alternatives such as rape oil, olive oil, seed oil, various fish oils and whale-blubber oil.

The need for lightships and light buoys arose because of sand-banks, which were not only obstacles but could also change their locations in shallow waters or river mouths. This was an obvious danger to vessels, particularly where tidal levels differed greatly. Lightships were probably first used off Holland's coast already in the 1400s. But the first known lightship was English, stationed at Nore Sands in the Thames estuary in 1732, and followed by several others along the coast of England during the 1780s.

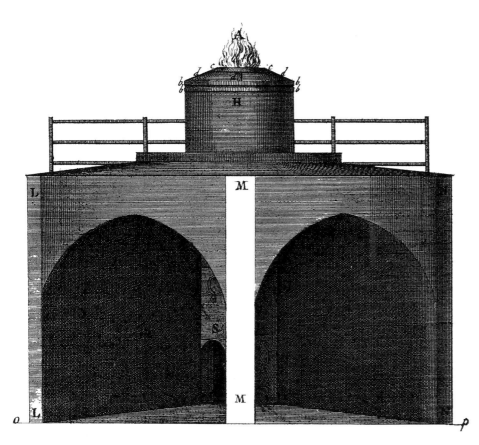

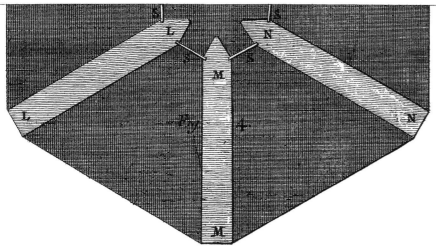

Coal was used increasingly in rebuilt fire-beacons, and in new lighthouses with glass lanterns and adjustable air channels that created a draught under the coal-grate to give a strong, white, smokeless flame. This new type of light was developed chiefly by the famous English lighthouse architect John Smeaton (1724-92), the Swedish engineer Anders Polheimer (1746-1811) and the Danish commodore Poul de Löwenörn (1751-1826). The coal light's glow made a reliable beacon and was thus more popular among seafarers than other new sophisticated lamp systems until the 1800s.

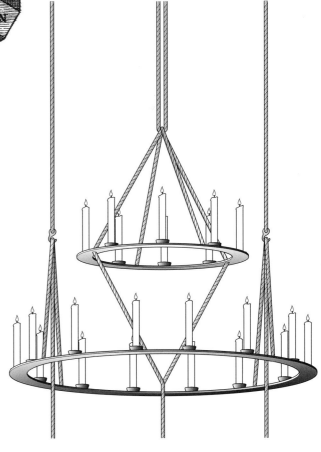

Wax lamps were still used by the churches, but too limited by their high cost and low availability for lighthouses in general. Tallow lamps were a cheaper alternative, yet they reeked and produced more smoke. Despite this, even sea-beacons employed tallow-lamp candelabras: Eddystone I (1699) had 60 candles and Eddystone III (1759-1807) was equipped with 24.

The 19th century brought better and relatively smoke-free choices: the stearine lamp, patented in 1825 by Michel Eugène Chevreul (1786-1889) in France, and the paraffin (kerosene) lamp which was first made in 1830 by Karl von Reichenbach in Germany. However, by this time other, stronger sources of illumination for lighthouses had been invented.

The French scientist Antoine Lavoisier, in 1765, showed that it was essential for the light source to be almost a point, and to lie at the reflector's focus, if the rays in a parabolic reflector were to be concentrated. In 1763-77 the first scientifically designed, large spherical and parabolic beacon reflectors were made by the harbour- master in Liverpool, William Hutchinson. The method was to make a wooden form, cast the reflector in plaster, and glue small reflectors of polished tin onto it. Once Hutchinson's method became known, many competing methods of making parabolic reflectors were developed in England, France and Germany. Two Frenchmen, M. Teulère and M. Lenoir, are thought to have been the first, around 1780, to manufacture parabolic reflectors of silvered copper.

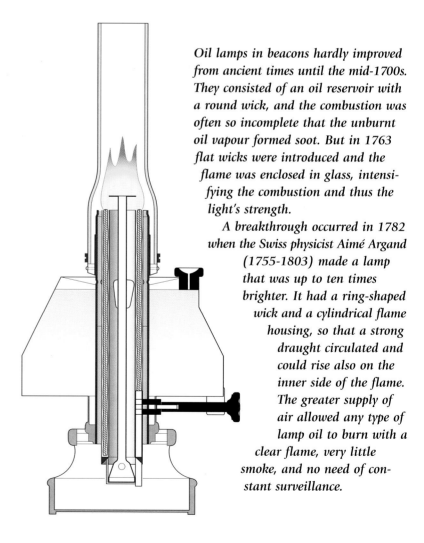

Around 1660 a Swede named Johan Daniel Braun designed and manufactured cast-steel mirrors for reflection in beacons, which he patented in 1681. The first Swedish lighthouses, at Landsort in 1669 and Örskär about 1685, had oil lamps with Braun's curved steel mirrors to direct and amplify the light. The reflectors probably had a parabolic shape, but this is uncertain as both of the lighthouses were wooden and burned down after a few decades, to be replaced with stone towers.

Örskar had five reflectors with six oil lamps each. Yet the light source was not as strong as predicted, since too many lamps were not in focus and diffused the light. Besides, the lamps created plenty of smoke that dimmed the light.

Oil lamps in beacons hardly improved from ancient times until the mid-1700s. They consisted of an oil reservoir with a round wick, and the combustion was often so incomplete that the unburnt oil vapour formed soot. But in 1763 flat wicks were introduced and the flame was enclosed in glass, intensifying the combustion and thus the light's strength.

A breakthrough occurred in 1782 when the Swiss physicist Aimé Argand (1755-1803) made a lamp that was up to ten times brighter. It had a ring-shaped wick and a cylindrical flame housing, so that a strong draught circulated and could rise also on the inner side of the flame. The greater supply of air allowed any type of lamp oil to burn with a clear flame, very little smoke, and no need of constant surveillance.

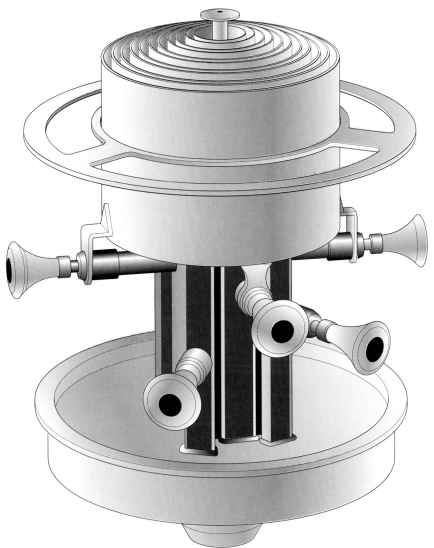

The Argand lamp was later refined by the French watch-maker Bertrand Carcel (1750-1812). In 1800 he designed a lamp with several concentric wicks, based on Argand's principle. He also made a weight-driven or clockwork-powered pump, which pressed the oil up through the wicks to provide a surplus of oil. This design was simplified by a Parisian, Franchot, into the moderator lamp, where the pump in the oil reservoir was replaced with spring pressure on the oil, and the oil supply to the wick was regulated by a needle valve.

For almost a century afterward, the multiple Argand-type burner with up to 10 concentric wicks – further developed by Benjamin Thompson (Count Rumford) (1753-1814), Francois Arago, and Augustin Jean Fresnel (1788-1827) – was the dominant source of illumination in lighthouses.

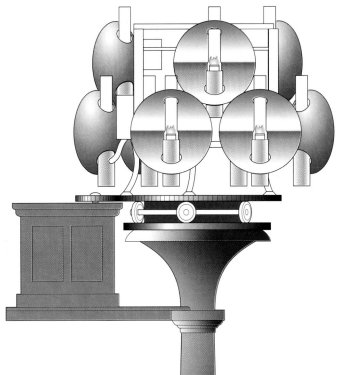

The desire to distinguish lights from each other by giving them different characteristics was first satisfied in Sweden by Jonas Norberg (1711-1783), who built a new type of beacon with rotating mirrors driven by a clockwork. Experiments with the method were carried out at the lighthouses of Korsö (1757) and Örskär (1768), using a hand-powered mechanism that turned the reflectors back and forth. The first rotating reflector-lamp system had three oil lamps with two reflectors each, and was driven by a weight. It was set up at the fortress of Carlsten in Marstrand and, for the first time, gave rhythmical changes between light and dark. Norberg's system was also used outside Sweden – initially at the lighthouses of Dieppe (1784) and Liverpool (1785), then at the Cordouan lighthouse where, in 1790, J. C. Borda and J. Teulère installed a similar system with about 30 lamps and reflectors.

Advances during the 1800s

As seafaring expanded in the early 19th century, steamships took over the sailing vessel's role increasingly, and many marine nations began to build chains of lighthouses along their coasts. Since steam power made ships faster and enabled them to steer independently of winds and tides, the need also grew for effective beacons that could be seen at distances of more than 20 nautical miles. New technology was required, too, for exact all-weather buoy-marking of sea lanes, which were used by night as well. After the advent of steel chains in the 1820s, floating lane-markers such as light-ships and buoys could be anchored to mark a lane's beginning and direction. Bell-buoys appeared in the 1860s and, a few decades later, gas-powered light buoys with a gas reservoir for about one month of operation.

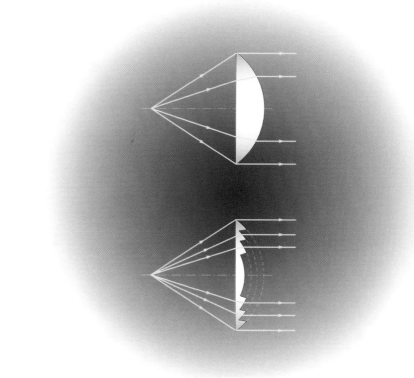

Fresnel was secretary of France's lighthouse commission and in 1820, on a contract from the Academy of Sciences, he designed the first "Fresnel lens", whose high yield of light began a new era in beacon development. This type of lens is still used today. One lens directs light toward the horizon and is surrounded by rings of prisms that catch the diffused light. The Fresnel lens was introduced in 1823 at the Cordouan lighthouse near Bordeaux, built with plane mirrors to refract the outermost rays toward the horizon.

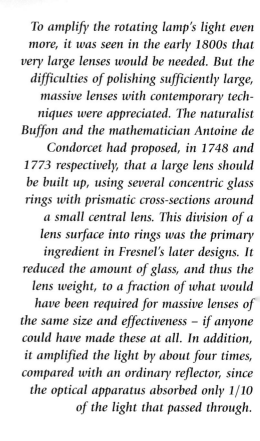

To amplify the rotating lamp's light even more, it was seen in the early 1800s that very large lenses would be needed. But the difficulties of polishing sufficiently large, massive lenses with contemporary techniques were appreciated. The naturalist Buffon and the mathematician Antoine de Condorcet had proposed, in 1748 and 1773 respectively, that a large lens should be built up, using several concentric glass rings with prismatic cross-sections around a small central lens. This division of a lens surface into rings was the primary ingredient in Fresnel's later designs. It reduced the amount of glass, and thus the lens weight, to a fraction of what would have been required for massive lenses of the same size and effectiveness – if anyone could have made these at all. In addition, it amplified the light by about four times, compared with an ordinary reflector, since the optical apparatus absorbed only 1/10 of the light that passed through.

Subsequently, Fresnel designed his other main type of beacon lens: the drum lens, for non-rotating light systems. It is a vertical cylinder of poured glass, in which lie several circular prismatic rings that refract the light from a source at the cylinder's centre. This type was first installed in 1825 at the French lighthouse of Chassiron.

Augustin Jean Fresnel (1788-1927)

The development of beacon optics was revolutionized by this French scientist's work. He studied physics at the Ecole Polytechnique and became an engineer at Ponts et Chausses, the road department, which also dealt with beacon activities in France. His experiments with optics began in 1816, and he won a prize in 1819 from the French Academy of Sciences for research on diffraction of light. When the government formed a special lighthouse commission, he was chosen as secretary by its chairman, Francois Arago. Under his direction, the Argand lamp and beacon optics were then developed. By 1822, Fresnel had created a lamelle lens which made possible the future's efficient beacon lenses, and which still exists today in various forms.

When Fresnel died at only 39, his lens system was already in use and being manufactured by, among others, his brother Leonor. It was later refined mainly in Britain by two brothers, Alan and Thomas, of the famous lighthouse family Stevenson.

The next step along Fresnel's path was to unite reflectors (catoptrics) with lenses and prisms (dioptrics) into a combined "catadioptric" system. This was essential for sea lights needing great power. Fresnel died in 1827, aged only 39 – but his brother Leonor made lenses in Paris and, in 1831, went to work for the optical manufacturer Cookson in Newcastle, England. There, Fresnel systems were built for fifteen English lighthouses until 1845.

During the 1850s, Fresnel's catadioptric systems were vastly improved by two Englishmen, Alan Stevenson and James Timmins Chance, at the optical company of Chance Brothers in Birmingham, founded in 1824. This firm remained the only manufacturer of such lighthouse optics in England until 1959. But the world market during the 19th century was dominated by French optical companies.

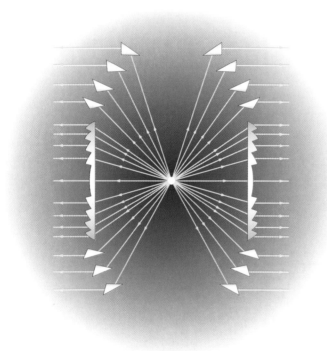

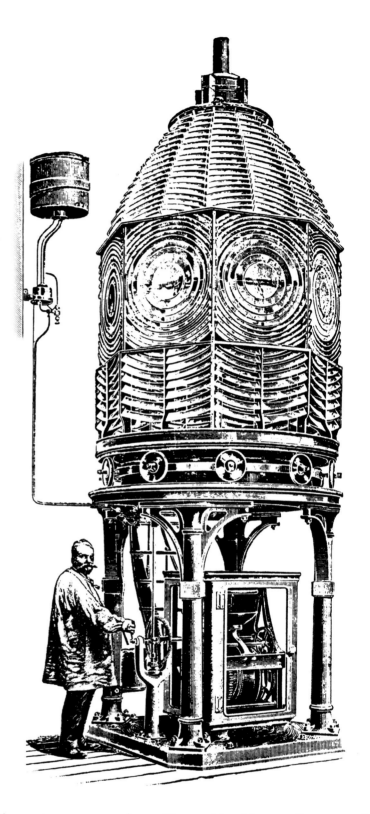

The biggest rotating Fresnel lens systems were very heavy. They could weigh up to five tons and, at first, rotated on simple roller-bearings. These had to support the system while turning it with a certain speed and little friction. All the force came from a weight-driven or hand-wound clockwork. For large lighthouse lenses, the bearing problem was solved by a Frenchman, Bourdelles. In 1890, he put the system on a ring-shaped float in a matching container filled with mercury. This enabled the rotation speed to be increased, creating a "flashing light". In later systems, the air draught from the lamp's heat was the only force needed to rotate such a low-friction apparatus.

Even so, oil products were still expensive and oil lamps need continuous supervision. Therefore, an effort was made to exploit the great investment in coal gas, which took place after it was developed by a Scot, William Murdoch (1754-1839), primarily for city lighting. In 1808 the lighthouse at Porkala, Finland, burned a gas extracted from wood. City gas could be produced in a local plant and transported by pipes; in 1818, it was also used as a fuel in the lighthouse of Salvatore at Trieste, Italy. A natural result was the idea of making lamps that shone continuously without daily attention.

During the first half of the 19th century, attempts were made to produce illuminating oil by distillation of coal (paraffin) and to extract mineral oils from various kinds of shale. Thus, when the oil industry's pioneer, Edwin Drake of Titusville, USA, first pumped up petroleum from bedrock in 1859, the oil-refining techniques already existed. Early in the 1860s, usable petroleum-based illuminating oils went onto the world market – mainly paraffin. The combination of paraffin with the Argand lamp quickly became the cheapest, most effective source of illumination in lighthouses.

The Douglass family

Nicholas Douglass came to the English light-house authority, Trinity House, as a designer in 1839. Among other things, he directed the building of Bishops Rock. His son, James Nicholas (1826-98), became chief engineer at Trinity House in 1863 and, holding this post for 29 years, built twenty large light-houses in the British Empire, including the famous granite tower on Eddystone Rock in 1882. James' brother William (1831-1923) worked at Trinity House for 26 years, and in 1878 became chief engineer of the Irish lighthouse authority for 20 years. James' son, William Tregarthen-Douglass, was the last representative in Trinity House of this family, which built a total of 28 lighthouses.

Julius Pintsch (1810-84), in Berlin, developed an oil gas in 1871 for railway lighting, and light buoys began to use it in 1879. Produced by distilling vegetable and mineral oils, it could be compressed to 1/10 of its volume in closed steel con-tainers. This allowed a buoy to be left unattended for months.

The first such light buoy was laid in the Thames estuary in 1880. For the next 15 years, over 400 Pintsch buoys were sold. Also in 1880, the lighthouse at Pillau in Poland became the first in the world to be equipped for unattended opera-tion. Its gas was supplied by a pipeline, 1 km long, from a Pintsch gas container on land. In 1894, an unmanned lightship, Rocheboune, was stationed on the French coast, and Pintsch gas was used in a series of such ships starting in 1900.

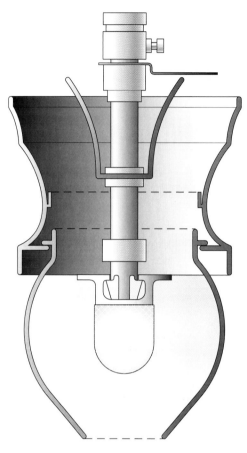

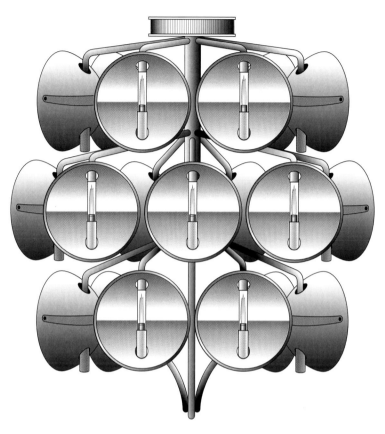

Now the efficiency of gas lights needed to be improved. An Austrian, Carl Auer von Welsbach (1858-1929), in 1885, presented an incandescent mantle, made of silk net coated with an earth metal. Fueled by coal gas and air, it gave a very strong flame. Thereafter, several new illuminating gases were developed that, together with the Auer net, became the most effective light sources in beacons, until the electric lamp began its triumphant career.

In 1811 an Englishman, Robert Stevenson (1772-1850), invented a mechanical device for mirror optics, with two cylindrical screens that made a light blink periodically. After the middle of the 19th century, lighthouse engineers in various countries developed further methods of producing distinctive lights, such as rotating screens and Venetian blinds. A proposal by the English scientist Sir William Thomson (Lord Kelvin) in the 1870s, to create characteristic Morse codes for different beacons, was considered by the authorities, but it proved technically impossible.

Other new fuels – such as Blau gas, compressible up to 100 times – were also used in lighthouses and buoys. But it was acetylene, a pure chemical compound of hydrogen and carbon, discovered in 1892, that contributed most to the invention of new beacons and buoys with illuminating gas. Its light strength was about 20 times greater than what ordinary gas could provide. One kilogram of calcium carbide yields 340 liters of acetylene gas, and this could be achieved locally by adding water.

While the lamps and their optics had reached satisfactory quality, the problem was how to recognize a light. At some places, several light towers were built adjacently. But after the Industrial Revolution, many fixed light sources existed on land that could be confused with a beacon – and a blinking light was hard to distinguish from the stars. Thus arose the need of a system for creating different light characters.

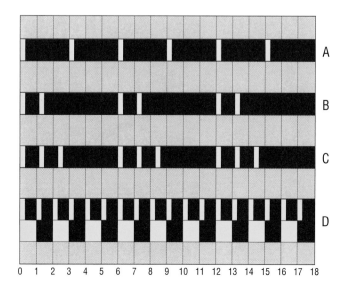

The Stevenson family

Robert Stevenson (1772-1850) was born in Glasgow and soon lost his father. He was taken care of and made an assistant by Thomas Smith, the only engineer at Scotland's lighthouse authority, the Commissioners of Northern Lighthouses. Thus began an era of management by three generations of Stevensons for more than 150 years. In all, they were responsible for building over 85 lighthouses.

Already in 1811, Robert directed the construction of Bell Rock Tower. By 1845, he had designed and built 15 large sea beacons. His oldest son Alan (1807-65), chief engineer from 1843 to 1853, built 12 lighthouses and developed the first occulting light, as well as optimizing Fresnel's lens system. Two brothers, David and Thomas, were lighthouse engineers for 30 years, during which they built 29 beacons. In the next generation, David Alan (1854-1938) accounted for 22 lighthouses. His own cousin, another David Alan (1891-1972), was the last in the family to work with lighthouses, and documented its activities.

Coastal shipping expanded so much in the 1800s that many invisible obstacles had to be marked with beacons, such as sand-banks and underwater shoals that a vessel could run aground on. The use of lightships was discouraged by the high cost of keeping their crews of 10-15 men at work in sometimes difficult conditions. Hence, new types of beacons that required little maintenance were developed to replace them. The first attempt had been made already in 1776 off the coast of Pembrokeshire in England, where the lighthouse of Smalls was built on piles of oak.

In Sweden, the coastal lighthouse chain was extended with 11 framework beacons between 1858 and 1874 – an investment that could not have been financed otherwise. Towards the end of the century, concrete also came into use and was soon the predominant material for lighthouses.

Earlier techniques of building lighthouses with stone blocks became too expensive in the mid-1800s. As the supply of iron increased rapidly and its cost declines, lighthouses began to be built of iron frameworks, whose elements could be specially manufactured for assembly on the spot. In England in 1840, a framework lighthouse was built with nine cast-iron screw piles on a sand-bank at Maplin Sands in the Thames estuary. The design was patented by an Irishman, Alexander Mitchell, around 1830. Some ten "open iron beacons" were built in England and the USA during the 1850s.

The Halpin family

A father and son, George Halpin Sr. and Jr., had charge of building more than 50 lighthouses in Ireland between 1812 and about 1860. When the father worked as harbour engineer at Dublin in 1810, he became involved in building beacons with the Commissioners of Irish Lighthouses. His son became an assistant in 1830, and the pair proceeded to construct many lighthouses together. George Halpin Jr. is best known as the designer and builder of the iron tower at Fastnet Rock in 1854 – the same year his father died.

The world's first caisson beacon was built in 1880 at Rothersand on the north coast of Germany, on sandbanks in the Weser river estuary, where the sea route for Atlantic steamers to Bremerhaven passed. A caisson was sunk by filling it with sand and, after much trouble and cost, a lighthouse was finally erected on the caisson and lit in 1995.

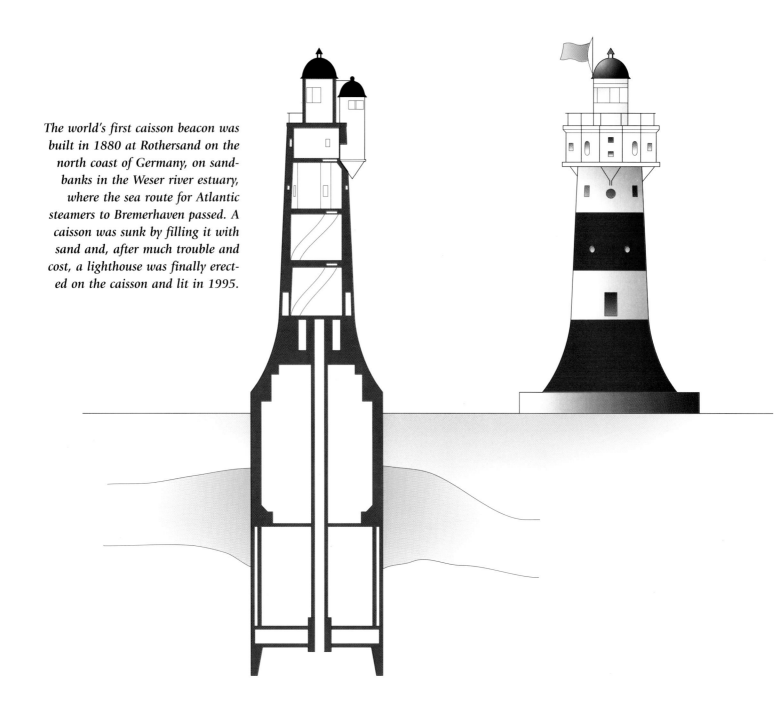

Inventions that revolutionized lighthouses

The successful gas glow-lamp, with its so-called Auer burner, ran straight into competition with the PVB – Pressurised Vapour Burner – developed by Arthur Kitson in 1901. This apparatus vaporizes the oil (paraffin or some other light mineral oil) by applying pressure and heat in tubes over the burner. Then the mantle is heated and lit, giving a flame with a light six times stronger than an ordinary mineral-oil lamp. Kitson's gas burner greatly decreased the need for oil gases that had recently been launched in lighthouse technology.

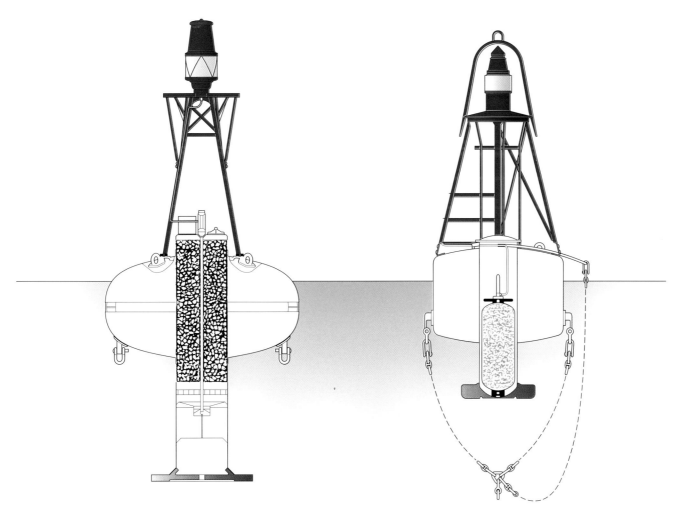

In 1892, Leopold Wilson in the USA, and Henri Moisson in France, had simultaneously discovered acetylene, which could be produced with calcium carbide and water. The news of this superb illuminating gas spread quickly but, when many countries put it into use, it turned out to be so explosive that it was very hard to transport and handle – especially if under pressure. Two Frenchmen, Georges Claude and Albert Hess, worked on the problem and invented "acetylene dissous" in 1896. This was a method of dissolving the gas in acetone, then filling the acetylene container with porous material to prevent an explosion. The method worked, but explosions still occurred due to hollows formed in the material.

Acetylene light buoys, where the gas was generated in the buoy, were introduced in 1904 by Willson in Canada. Many such buoys were sold in Canada and South America, but the system proved unreliable. There were accidental explosions, and when the water froze, the buoy was extinguished.

A clear advance toward modern illumination took place when the National Swedish Administration of Pilotage, Lighthouses and Buoys started to use acetylene as a fuel in beacons. The lighthouse at Marstrand was given acetylene lighting in 1900, and in 1902 some light buoys with their own gas plants were laid out. They were expected to operate unattended for one month, but problems soon arose. Instead, a test was made with light buoys using "acetylene dissous". To solve further problems, the administration's chief engineer, John Höjer (1849-1908), handed the project to a new company, AGA. While the acetylene flame's strength was more than sufficient, the gas consumption was so great that continuous operation became too expensive.

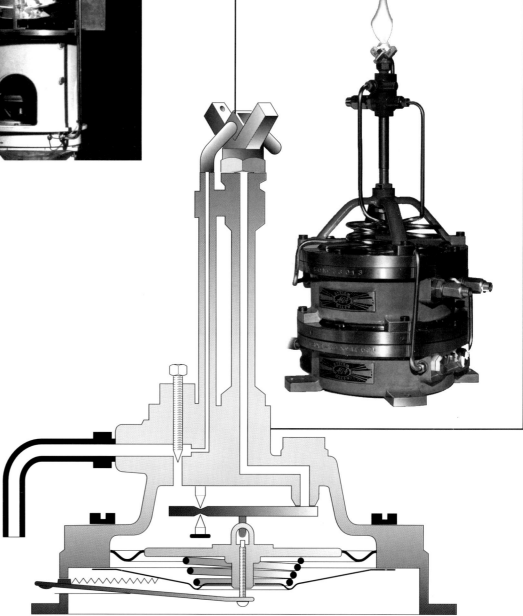

John Höjer argued that, if acetylene was to have any future in lighthouses, it must be made completely safe and a device must be found that used less gas, besides creating specific character-istics for the light. In other words, a blinker light was needed. This task fell upon Gustaf Dalén (1869-1937), a consultant engineer at AGA. In 1906 he managed to design an occulting device that could emit very short flashes of light and worked unexpectedly well. With a gas saving of 90% and flexible light characters, Dalén could devote himself to the problem of safety.

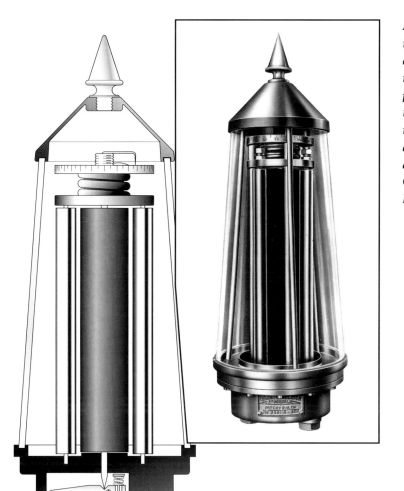

AGA developed a new, improved porous material with small capillaries, for containers using the "acetylene dissous" method. This enabled the gas, with no risk of explosion, to be transported under pressure to lighthouses and buoys. Additional savings were possible, and Dalén realized that beacons need not shine during the day. He thought of building a solar valve, based on the differing expansion of certain metals when influenced by sunlight and daylight. The valve decreased the gas consumption by nearly half, and was first installed at the lighthouse of Furuholmen in 1907. Gustaf Dalén's invention earned him the 1912 Nobel Prize in Physics.

Gustaf Dalén had now developed the first light system that could operate for a long time without attention. But large lighthouses still required supervision because the mantle soon burned up. Thus in 1916, Dalén – despite having gone blind in 1912 – invented the mantle changer, which could automatically replace a burned-out mantle with a new one. Given a magazine of 24 mantles, a lighthouse was able to operate by itself for more than a year.

Large lighthouses at sea required the highest possible light strength, and therefore used gas in combination with mantles, on the principle of Auer von Welsbach. The optimum gas mixture with a mantle was one part of acetylene to ten parts of air, which is very explosive. But in 1909 came the Dalén blender, which mixed the gas in the right proportions with no risk of explosion, regardless of the external conditions. Later, it also proved able to generate power for rotating the lens system. Such lighthouses had long used rotating lenses that were driven by a clockwork with weights, which had to be raised at least every sixth hour. To eliminate the need for lighthouse crews, Dalén was forced to automate the lens rotation – otherwise the automatic mantle device would be pointless. In 1917 the rotation apparatus was ready, based on the Dalén blender's membrane movements.

On lightships, there was the problem that a fixed lens system, which moves along with the vessel, casts the light up and down. This was solved by Dalén in 1915 with the "lens pendulum". The lens system had a gimbal mounting at its centre of gravity and was connected by draw-lines with a stabilization point at the vessel's centre of motion.

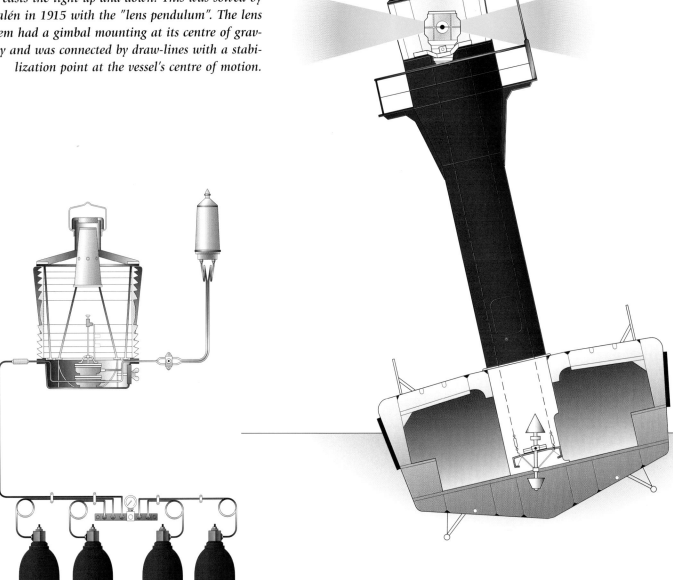

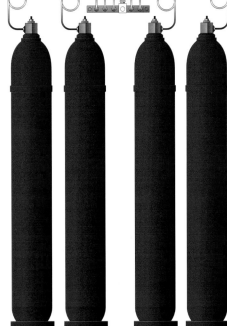

Dalén's inventions, which made up the AGA system, were highly reliable. They could operate unattended for a year and without complete maintenance for up to 20 years. The possibility of fully automatic lighthouse operation using no electricity gave the system a fast start on the world market, and it also served as a back-up system in electrical lighthouses for many decades.

Nils Gustaf Dalén was born on 30 November 1869 at Stenstorp, Väster-götland, Sweden, the third of five children of a farmer. His parents, having no savings and supported only by their farm, gave all the children good educations. Gustaf soon showed practical talent, but was somewhat lazy in school and, therefore, was considered the most suitable of the children to take over the farm. Sent to a folk high-school and a farmers' school, he was trained especially in dairy techniques.

From childhood to life as a young farmer, Dalén constantly solved technical problems. One invention was to change his future. While working in the farm's dairy, he noticed that the milk can vary in fat content. Since he thought that the fat content should determine the milk price, he made an apparatus to measure it. In 1891, he took the device to Stockholm and approached Gustaf de Laval, world-famous inventor of the milk separator. Dalén was disappointed to find that Laval had recently sought a patent on a fat tester which was quite like his own. But on Laval's advice, he decided to give up farming and become an engineer.

In 1892, he began to study at Chalmers Technical College in Göteborg, finishing four years later with a brilliant diploma. After a year of further study at the Polytechnicum in Zürich, he went to work for Laval. Now he grew interested in Laval's efforts with acetylene and, together with a fellow student named Henrik von Celsing, started a company to introduce acetylene lighting. Later he was employed by the Swedish Carbide and Acetylene Company, which in 1904 became AB Gasaccumulator (AGA).

AGA

This company began to manufacture acetylene gas, dis-

Gustaf Dalén (1869-1937)

covered rather recently, and to exploit the French invention of distributing acetylene for illumination by dissolving it in acetone under pressure in gas bottles. The new company made use of Gustaf Dalén's services as a consultant engineer. His inventions in lighthouse technology became the key to AGA's development, and from the beginning of 1906 he worked only for AGA as chief engineer. The business expanded quickly and, when AGA was reorganized in 1909, Dalén became its Managing Director.

The AGA premises in Stockholm were soon too small, and on Lidingö Island – then linked to the mainland only by a pontoon bridge – more land was bought to build new factories. These were occupied by the staff of 150 in 1912, when AGA received an order for all the beacons and light buoys in the Panama Canal. This large order brought the company fame and a world-wide market.

Gustaf Dalén was blinded by an acetylene accident in late 1912, but he continued to direct and develop AGA until his death in 1937. His work included:
• Expanding the manufacture of beacons to provide all kinds of aids for traffic by sea, land and air.
• Improvement of welding to become an essential tool for industry and crafts.
• Production of oxygen gas, and refinement of occulting valves, which led in time to development of medical techniques.
• Radio and sound film production in the subsidiary company Aga-Baltic, which was founded in 1930 and, from 1933, directed by Dalén's son Gunnar. This activity resulted in manufacture of advanced electronics and optics.

In 1912, Gustaf Dalén received the Nobel Prize in Physics for his basic design of the solar valve.

From gas and oil to electricity

The first electric lamps were used as beacon sources from 1884 onward in some small, unmanned French lighthouses. Their current was generated by galvanic elements, but their filaments were too small to suit the existing optical systems. As a result, acetylene and PVB burners entirely predominated in lighthouses until after World War I. Still, the light bulb had a luminosity up to ten times greater than the PVB burner, and an effective intensity much higher than what would be needed in modern lighthouses.

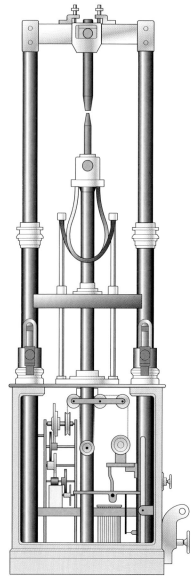

On a recommendation by the famous English physicist Michael Faraday, electricity was first used in the form of a carbon-arc lamp at the English lighthouses of Holmes (1857) and Dungerness (1862). Initially, this very bright arc was believed to be the best solution for beacons. But it soon proved difficult to maintain and unreliable, and produced a carbon dust that dirtied lenses and lantern panes. The lamp's light-element was also quite small and, therefore, unsuitable as a source for older lens systems, which were not manufactured with enough precision. Hence, the lamp had to be provided with special prismatic optical systems. And the construction costs were enormous, as such lighthouses needed their own coal- or steam-powered electricity plants.

The electrification of lighthouses could not get under way until the electricity distribution network was expanded significantly in the early 20th century. But even then, supervision was needed due to power failures and burned-out bulbs. So the lighthouses were given a "light shunter" with a burner having a reserve supply of acetylene gas. This was coupled in automatically with the same occulting light that the electric lamp had, if the latter went out.

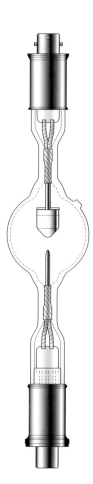

Most of the shift from gas to electricity occurred after World War II. The xenon-arc lamp, introduced in 1947, had an unsurpassed light density. Since it contained gas at high pressure and required very strong current, as well as 10-kV high-voltage pulses to start, it could explode and was therefore not a direct successor to the gas lamp. Small xenon-discharge lamps with short light bursts have thus been used only in lightships with ranges up to 21 nautical miles.

Ranges of different beacon lamps

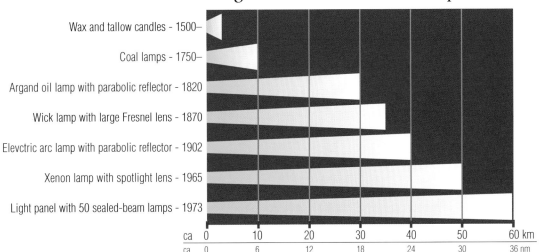

Wax and tallow candles - 1500–							
Coal lamps - 1750–							
Argand oil lamp with parabolic reflector - 1820							
Wick lamp with large Fresnel lens - 1870							
Elevctric arc lamp with parabolic reflector - 1902							
Xenon lamp with spotlight lens - 1965							
Light panel with 50 sealed-beam lamps - 1973							

ca	0	10	20	30	40	50	60 km
ca	0	6	12	18	24	30	36 nm

In the mid-1950s, as an alternative to electrical wire-filament lamps in lens systems, a matrix of rotating spotlights of the "sealed beam" type was installed on fixed beacons built to replace lightships. Each lamp unit has a parabolic reflector with a halogen lamp element placed exactly at the focus. The module has a very high yield of light with little diffusion, and the desired light strength can be achieved by arranging the lamps in groups. When renovating old beacons, earlier light sources and optics were usually replaced with a lamp module of the desired strength.

The Fifties saw a gradual decline of acetylene and propane systems in favour of battery-powered electrical devices. The occulting function differs in that, while the gas flame is lit and extinguished immediately, the filament lamp needs a short time to warm up and cool down. The latter's lifetime is about 1,000 hours, whereas gas burners work unattended for several years. With low-power bulbs, the optics used were often made of moulded plastic instead of polished glass. Exploitation of new electrical energy sources such as solar cells, wind generators, and nuclear plants for operating lighthouses has recently led to rapid automation and much lower costs.

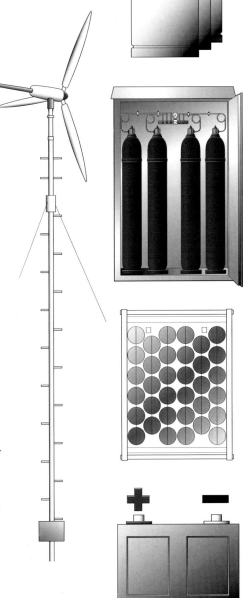

New methods of building light-houses

In the years after World War II, many sea beacons were given new equipment that demanded a supply of electricity with diesel-powered generators. The lighthouses normally contained electric lamps with reserve gas, as well as fog-signal and radio-beacon apparatuses. Often the first step toward automation was taken by making the beacons semi-automatic, that is, with alarms and back-up systems that took care of acute problems before the personnel could fix them. The next step was to render a beacon unmanned. It was then controlled and checked entirely by radio from another, still manned lighthouse. The last step was to co-ordinate all lighthouses' surveillance systems in a national centre.

Once lighthouses became unmanned, there was great difficulty in bringing personnel quickly out to a lighthouse for urgent repair of faults and for routine inspection. Lennart Hallengren (1926-79), a Head of Division of the National Swedish Board of Shipping and Navigation, solved this problem during the 1960s by providing lighthouses with a helicopter landing pad on top. A demonstration occurred in a storm for the delegates to the IALA congress in Stockholm in 1970. Soon afterward, helicopter landings were introduced at many lighthouses in different parts of the world.

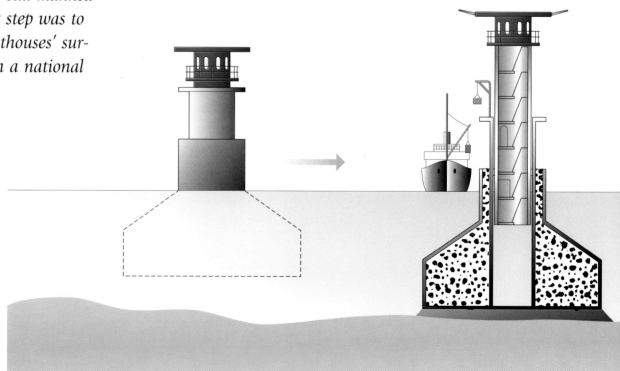

From the 1960s onward, lighthouse personnel became ever fewer as a result of technical progress. Beacons were increasingly automated and remote-controlled, while caisson beacons substituted for lightships. Pilotage and beacon sites closed down, and many people disappeared from places of work that had been manned for hundreds of years along coasts.

New construction methods were developed for sea lights during the 1950s. In the North and Baltic Seas, the Swedish pilotage administration then had 14 manned lightships to warn against dangerous underwater shoals. Their replacement with beacons was desired because of the high personnel costs (12-14 men per ship). This led to the "telescope" method of construction, patented by the Swedish lighthouse engineer Robert Gellerstad (1905-64). A beacon was completely built, equipped at the quay, and towed to its position in a caisson, floating like a vessel. There, the caisson was sunk, anchored and filled with ballast. The tower was lifted to the right height and cemented to the outer caisson, which was finally filled with macadam and sand. This method won international acceptance, and was used in Sweden to build 28 lighthouses between 1957 and 1987 – half of them replacing the last lightships.

A similar type of telescopic beacon, with a large deck at a low level, was designed and built in England by Sir William Halcrow & Partners in 1971, when the lightship at Royal Sovereign was to be replaced.

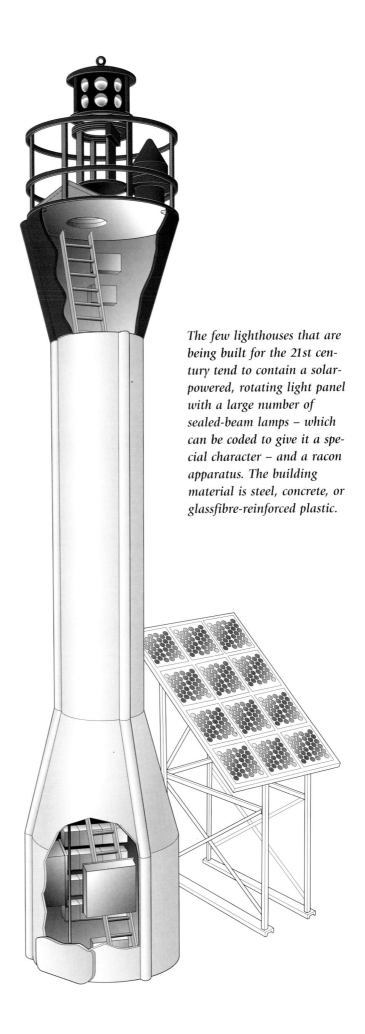

The few lighthouses that are being built for the 21st century tend to contain a solar-powered, rotating light panel with a large number of sealed-beam lamps – which can be coded to give it a special character – and a racon apparatus. The building material is steel, concrete, or glassfibre-reinforced plastic.

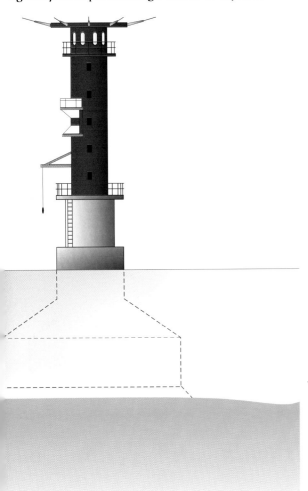

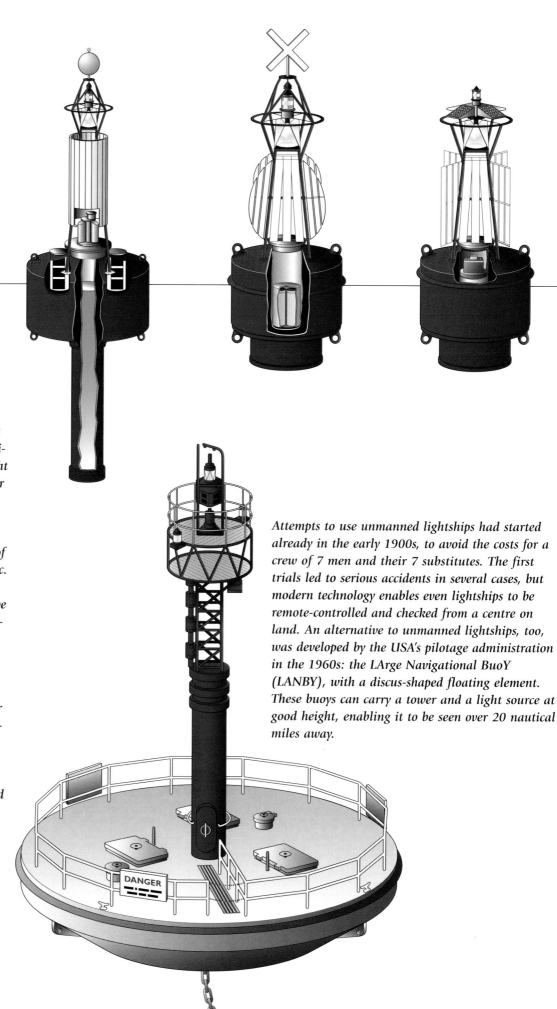

Since Pintsch, Willson, Dalén and others, around 1900, had developed light sources with supply systems that could be left unattended for long periods, a sizable market grew up for light buoys. The need was increased further by the huge expansion in seafaring with heavier tonnage and higher speeds. Ports became more crowded and there were ever-rising demands of safety and precision in harbour traffic. When battery-powered electric lamps replaced gas lamps, the buoys could be made less heavy, and great simplifications in design made them cheaper. Beginning in the 1960s, buoys were usually manufactured of glassfibre-reinforced plastic and, in addition to battery power, solar cells and wind or wave energy came into use for supplying the lamps with electricity. Lamp shunters could automatically change faulty bulbs up to six times. In the 1970s, compact fluorescent lamps and light diodes were also adopted for buoys.

Attempts to use unmanned lightships had started already in the early 1900s, to avoid the costs for a crew of 7 men and their 7 substitutes. The first trials led to serious accidents in several cases, but modern technology enables even lightships to be remote-controlled and checked from a centre on land. An alternative to unmanned lightships, too, was developed by the USA's pilotage administration in the 1960s: the LArge Navigational BuoY (LANBY), with a discus-shaped floating element. These buoys can carry a tower and a light source at good height, enabling it to be seen over 20 nautical miles away.

Navigation in fog and mist

Around 1900, navigational aids for poor visibility were very crude. It might have been thought that a strong arc lamp could penetrate through mist, but this was soon realized to be impossible. The only option was to transmit sounds, as had been done ever since ancient times.

Many different types of sound signals had been developed during the 19th century. Even these aids were unreliable, as mist has a phenomenal ability to dampen sound radiation and make it impossible to determine the distance or direction to the source. So there was great relief when, around World War I, radio communication became feasible between ships, and between them and lighthouses. With the arrival of electricity at lighthouses, much stronger sound signals could be transmitted as well.

To aid navigation over short distances, various sorts of sound signals (whistles, percussion devices, horns) have probably been used for as long as beacons themselves. At the Swedish lighthouse of Nidingen, for example, a special tower was built in 1766 with a bell that was rung four times every half hour in mist. Used until 1883, the Nidingen bell was probably the world's first land-based mist-signal station. The next known beacon with a mist signal was Bell Rock in England, which had two bells in 1811. Around 1735, the first English lightships were also equipped with fog From the first half of the 19th century onward, bells, gong-gongs, rockets, cannon shots, and detonations were used. During the 1850s, lighthouses began to acquire percussion mechanisms driven by steam or compressed air, and the first bell-buoys appeared in 1860.

Typical ranges of different fog/mist signals

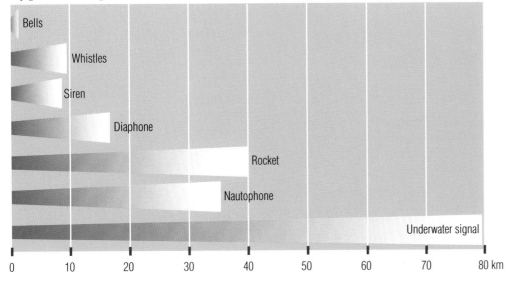

Bells
Whistles
Siren
Diaphone
Rocket
Nautophone
Underwater signal

0   10   20   30   40   50   60   70   80 km

How to create optimum mist signals became a subject of discussion in England and the USA
during the 1840s. In both countries, commissioners were appointed to make comparative
tests. The Americans recommended "Daboll's fog-horn",
invented by C. J. Daboll around
1850. It was a trumpet 5 metres
long, driven by steam or compressed air, with a 25-cm-long
"steel tongue" in the end. Such
"reed horns" were made stan-
dard equipment at lighthouses
in the USA, one of which, in
Boston, received a horn 12
metres long in 1890.

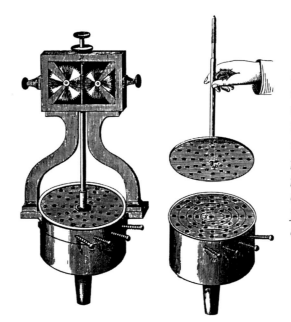

In England, after trials with steam-dri-
ven whistles and horns, a steam siren
was decided upon in 1862. Developed
by Frederick Holmes and George Slight,
it was patented by the American company Brown Brothers. Steam passed
perpendicularly through two perforated
discs, one rotating fast and the other
fixed, to create a sound whose tone
depended on the rotation speed.

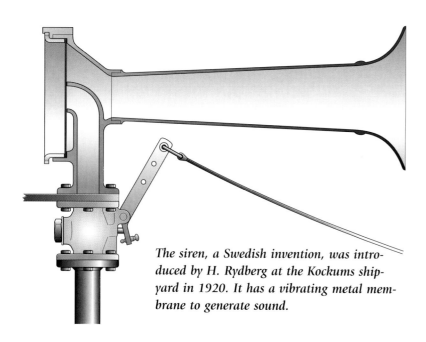

The siren, a Swedish invention, was introduced by H. Rydberg at the Kockums shipyard in 1920. It has a vibrating metal membrane to generate sound.

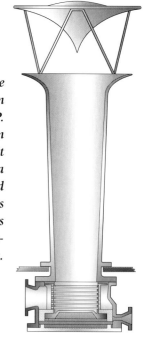

The diaphone
was invented in
1903 by Joseph P.
Nothey in
Canada. It
worked like a
siren but had
perforated pistons
and cylinders
instead of perfo-
rated discs.

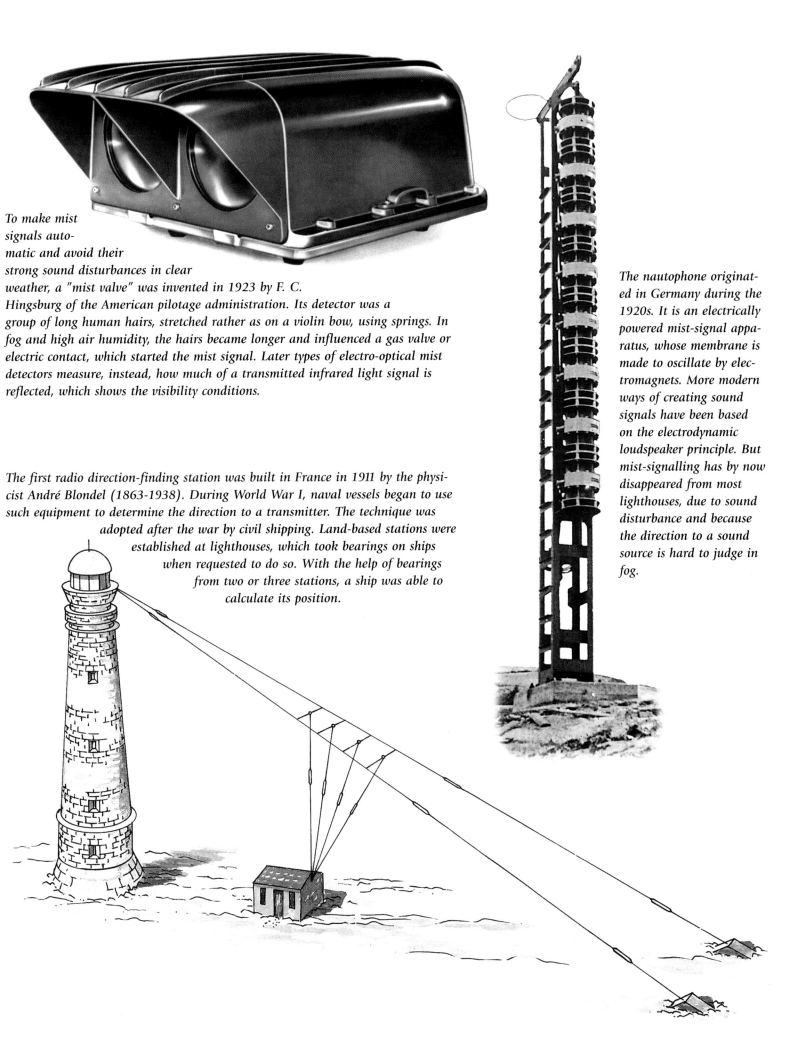

To make mist signals automatic and avoid their strong sound disturbances in clear weather, a "mist valve" was invented in 1923 by F. C. Hingsburg of the American pilotage administration. Its detector was a group of long human hairs, stretched rather as on a violin bow, using springs. In fog and high air humidity, the hairs became longer and influenced a gas valve or electric contact, which started the mist signal. Later types of electro-optical mist detectors measure, instead, how much of a transmitted infrared light signal is reflected, which shows the visibility conditions.

The first radio direction-finding station was built in France in 1911 by the physicist André Blondel (1863-1938). During World War I, naval vessels began to use such equipment to determine the direction to a transmitter. The technique was adopted after the war by civil shipping. Land-based stations were established at lighthouses, which took bearings on ships when requested to do so. With the help of bearings from two or three stations, a ship was able to calculate its position.

The nautophone originated in Germany during the 1920s. It is an electrically powered mist-signal apparatus, whose membrane is made to oscillate by electromagnets. More modern ways of creating sound signals have been based on the electrodynamic loudspeaker principle. But mist-signalling has by now disappeared from most lighthouses, due to sound disturbance and because the direction to a sound source is hard to judge in fog.

Heinrich Rudolf Hertz (1857-94)

Hertz was born in Hamburg on 22 February 1857. His father was a successful lawyer of Jewish origin, and his mother's father was a famous doctor in Frankfurt am Main. Heinrich's great talents appeared at a very early age, and he intended to become a building engineer. He began to study this subject at the Polytechnicum of Dresden in 1876, but stopped to do military service and, in 1877, continued at the Technical College in Munich, where he took up his favourite subjects of theoretical physics and mathematics.

Next he went to the Friedrich Wilhelm University in Berlin, and soon associated himself with Hermann von Helmholtz. In 1880 he took his doctorate with a dissertation on electromagnetic induction in rotating conductors, and in 1885 he became a professor of physics at the Technical College in Karlsruhe.

In 1888 he discovered radio ("Hertz") waves. Nikola Tesla tried as early as 1893 to use these waves for wireless transmission of information. Then an Italian, Guglielmo Marconi (1874-1937), invented the applications of Hertz waves that made radio a new field of technology.

Hertz met a tragic end. After becoming professor in 1885, he suffered from toothache, but was treated wrongly several times. In 1889 he had all his teeth pulled out, resulting in abscesses and much pain, and finally an operation. He was forced to stop working in the summer of 1893, and on 1 January 1894 he died of blood poisoning, only 36 years old. Yet the basis he laid for the techniques of radio and radar was to be a great blessing for seafarers.

Soon, though, a better method arose: the sea radio-beacon system, with transmitters that sent a Morse-code identification signal from different beacons and lightships. A ship carried a radio receiver with a rotatable antenna, allowing it to determine the directions to such beacons. The first radio beacon was set up in 1921 on the lightship "Ambrose" at the entrance to New York harbour.

During the 1930s, an international network of omnidirectional radio beacons was built up, enabling a ship to take bearings on them. Until the mid-1970s, there were also directional beacons – transmitters that gave a course line in a certain direction. In the 1970s and 1980s, however, hyperbolic and satellite navigation systems became the most common aids to merchant ships, so the radio-beacon system is going out of use. But some radio beacons will still be used to send dGPS (differential Global Positioning System) signals, which are corrections to increase the positional accuracy of satellite receivers.

In 1841, J. D. Colladon made experiments in Lake Geneva to test the radiation of sound signals in water. He managed to receive sound waves transmitted through water over more than 30 kilometres. Underwater mist-signalling employs the difference in speed between sound waves in water and those in air. A station sends strong sounds at the same time above and below water. Sensitive microphones above and below the waterline on a ship detect the signals, allowing calculation of the distance and direction to the source. This method was first used during World War I at distances up to 20 km. Once radio beacons were developed in the 1920s, a radio signal was sent out at the same time as the "water-mist" signal.

Modern aids to navigation

There was much improvement of navigational systems during World War II, with the invention of radar and of the "hyperbolic" navigation systems Consol, Decca Loran, and Omega. Hyperbolic navigation is based upon measuring the time difference in reception between two signals sent simultaneously from separate stations. All points with the same time difference lie on a pair of hyperbolic curves with the stations at their foci. Which signal is lagging shows which curve the ship lies on. A new measurement with two other stations gives a similar curve, and the intersection of these two curves is the ship's position. Its latitude and longitude are indicated directly by a "navigator" instrument, and further information can be obtained such as "waypoints" and the course.

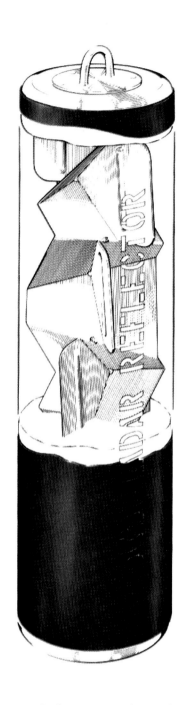

In the late 1940s, when radar was installed on merchant vessels, reflectors were mounted that strengthened the radar echo from fixed objects (including buoys and beacons) as well as movable ones (for instance, fishing boats and life rafts). This contributed greatly to radar's effectiveness as an aid to navigation in fog. Since then, radar has been steadily improved and provided with helpful systems such as an automatic warning of collision risk (ARPA).

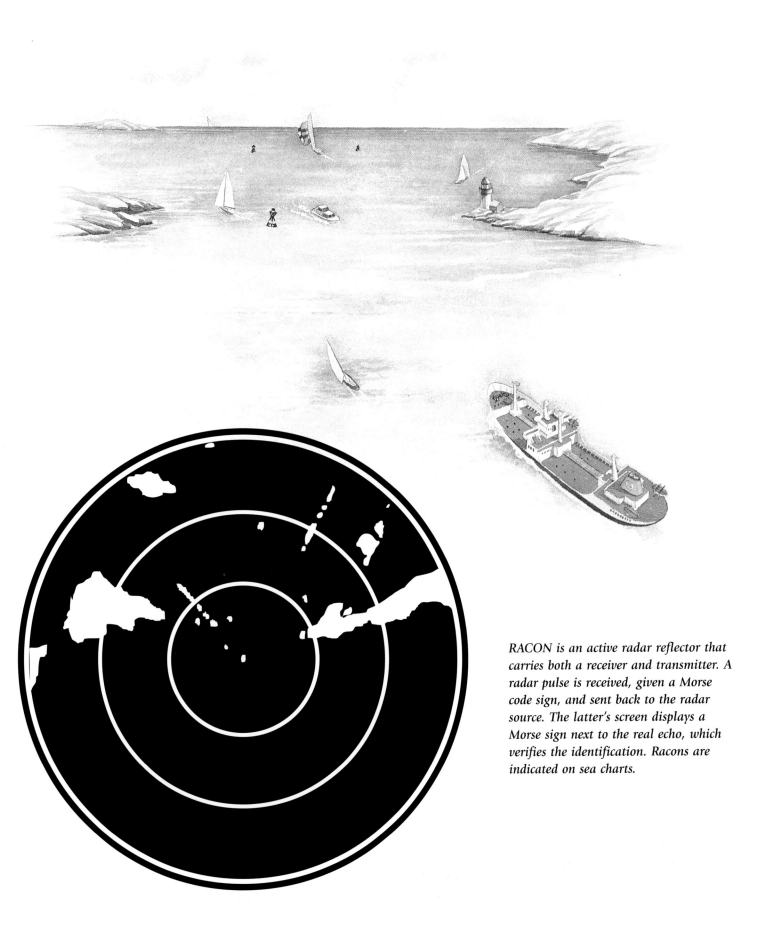

RACON is an active radar reflector that carries both a receiver and transmitter. A radar pulse is received, given a Morse code sign, and sent back to the radar source. The latter's screen displays a Morse sign next to the real echo, which verifies the identification. Racons are indicated on sea charts.

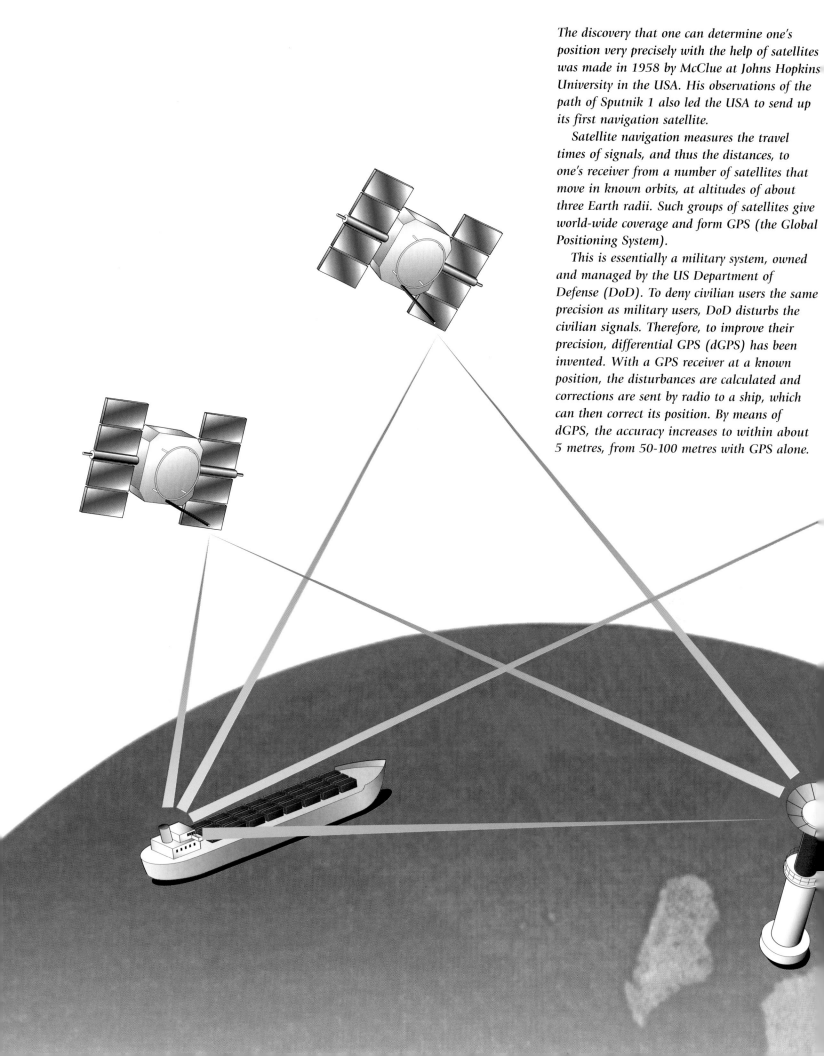

The discovery that one can determine one's position very precisely with the help of satellites was made in 1958 by McClue at Johns Hopkins University in the USA. His observations of the path of Sputnik 1 also led the USA to send up its first navigation satellite.

Satellite navigation measures the travel times of signals, and thus the distances, to one's receiver from a number of satellites that move in known orbits, at altitudes of about three Earth radii. Such groups of satellites give world-wide coverage and form GPS (the Global Positioning System).

This is essentially a military system, owned and managed by the US Department of Defense (DoD). To deny civilian users the same precision as military users, DoD disturbs the civilian signals. Therefore, to improve their precision, differential GPS (dGPS) has been invented. With a GPS receiver at a known position, the disturbances are calculated and corrections are sent by radio to a ship, which can then correct its position. By means of dGPS, the accuracy increases to within about 5 metres, from 50-100 metres with GPS alone.

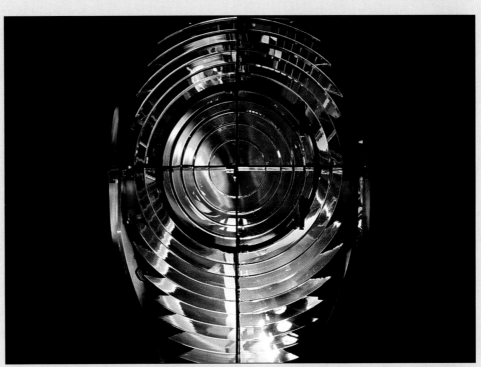

Throughout the Western world, during the past 50 years, lighthouse administrations have experienced more or less the same rapid technical progress, with automation and de-manning. The need for long-shining beacons and radio beacons that cover whole coasts has disappeared for professional seafarers. Few of these, however, want beacons to be extinguished, since the new complicated navigational aids can also break down, or be put out of action by a conflict. Lighthouses will continue to enhance safe sailing in our coastal waters and harbours, where both the container-ship captain and the fisherman still prefer to rely on their eyes and radar, rather than on "the eye in the sky".

The manned lighthouse also had an important humanitarian function – fast rescue for ships and small boats that got in trouble. Pleasure boaters could feel safer and had the chance to experience a genuine, living environment even in the outer coastal waters. Although some beacons must be extinguished, most of the interesting old lighthouse buildings will go on standing. For one thing, they are too expensive to destroy. Today, all over the world, non-profit lighthouse associations are being formed for the sole purpose of preserving lighthouses and their exciting history for posterity. In short, this is a unique part of our cultural heritage.

Lighthouse architecture

Many of the earliest lighthouses were originally built as unlit markers, but were later provided with illumination and thus came to be called lighthouses. Their basic task was to light the way for seafarers at night. If a marker or lighthouse was to be visible at very great distances, it had to be raised or situated high above the water surface. This was what gave birth to the lighthouse tower and has united architects around the world in the challenge of designing and erecting durable, well-working and beautiful lighthouses.

To understand the architecture of lighthouses, one must take account partly of direct influences such as the lighthouse's purpose, the lighting technology, building materials and location – and partly of indirect factors such as the prevailing social order and architectural styles. In addition, there is the need to use the lighthouse in further ways than illumination: for example, as a lookout and defence tower, a sanctuary, or a residence for the lighthouse personnel. If these aspects were absent when planning a lighthouse, it was usually just a technical structure with little artistic ambition. If a lighthouse served as a harbour beacon for a city, however, it was often given a more expensive appearance.

The first light-houses

Sea markers and beacons were probably first built by the Phoenicians, among the first seafaring peoples in the Mediterranean, between about 1200 and 300 BC. The Classical Greeks and Romans continued this tradition and set up many beacons, both in that sea and as far away as the English Channel. For none of these beacons do we know exact details as to their design, architecture and other possible functions. One point of special interest is the likelihood that they were a source of inspiration for the oldest minarets of Islamic mosques.

The Tower of Hercules at La Coruña, Spain, was built around AD 100 with a quadratic plan. In late Roman times the tower fell into ruin, and the following period of the early Middle Ages became a dark chapter in the history of lighthouses, as they were neglected due to the decline of trade and seafaring. But this tower was to be repaired and put back into use during the 17th century. Its completion above the quadratic wall resulted from changes and additions in the 1700s and 1800s.

The lighthouse at Genoa, called La Lanterna, was rebuilt in the 1540s. Its plan is quadratic, with a terrace in the middle supported by double corbelled friezes. The tower's upper part terminates in a corresponding manner. This design presumably derived from the original tower here, as it would otherwise have been more like the Renaissance forms that prevailed later on. For example, we may compare the 14th-century tower on the town hall in Siena with the lighthouse built at Cordouan during the late 16th century.

Similar towers arose in several medieval Italian city-states, but were then combined with other functions such as surveillance, defence or clock-towers. The tower at Genoa, too, was part of the city's defence.

Already in the 12th century, a new social order developed and shipping began to revive, once again initially around the Mediterranean Sea. Progress soon spread to northern Europe, where new trading ports and cities were founded. Near Genoa and Pisa (Meloria), for instance, towers that combined defence and illumination were built, which no longer exist today.

The medieval defensive lighthouse at Meloria was destroyed as late as 1944 during World War II, but it was reconstructed in 1956 and gives us an idea of how a fortified lighthouse from that age could look. The tower is 52 metres high, with a circular plan, divided in the middle by a narrow terrace and provided with crenellations. These also occur on the more slender upper part of the tower.

In Siena the town hall, or Palazzo Pubblico, was built during 1297-1348. Its clock-tower has a design that is seen many times in the history of lighthouses. The plan is quadratic, the walls are smooth, and the magnificent top has a terrace carried by a high corbelled frieze, in this case with pointed arches and completed by crenellations

The junction between the tower wall and the terrace – no matter whether the latter was square or round – often made use of a corbelled frieze that helped to bear up the terrace, but sometimes was simply a decoration. This is true of towers designed by architects, engineers and masterbuilders alike. The frieze could vary in form. Most common was the oldest type, consisting of stones cut in right angles or with only a slight profile. But the Romanesque semicircular arch was also used frequently.

Lighthouses in classical style

There are two parallel tendencies in the history of building lighthouses: the purely functional structure, and the architectural design that was functional as well. It was not unusual for an architect to be the building contractor as well – or vice versa. But gradually the construction work was specialized and, since lighthouses mainly had the technical function of illumination, the task was ever more often taken by engineers. The 19th century saw a widening gap between the craft of engineering and the artistic creativity of architecture. Function and, most importantly, economics became leading factors in planning, which also led to new ideals of style.

It has been common to make no particular architectural demands and give priority to the functions. Consequently, most lighthouses throughout the ages have been rather simple constructions. We shall thus review, instead, some lighthouses and proposed designs where the architectural ambitions have been relatively high. Moreover, quite a few famous architects have designed lighthouses even though not many of these have been built.

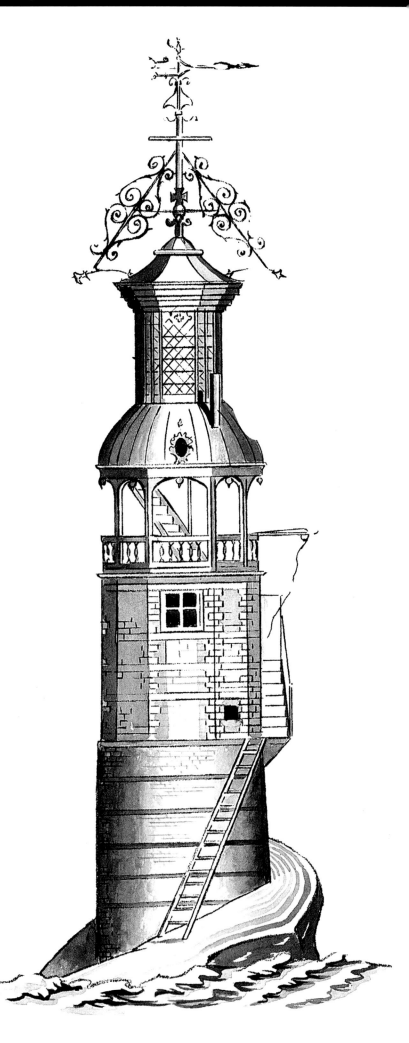

Especially remarkable is the history of the lighthouses on the famous Eddystone Rock, outside the port of Plymouth on the southeast coast of England. The first of its four beacons was built in 1696-98 on the initiative of Henry Winstanley, a shipowner with many pursuits. In spite of the difficult access to the rock, Winstanley did not hesitate to pay for a beautiful architectural design. The open terrace was crowned by a rounded roof, resting on posts connected by carved arches. On the roof was a lovely wooden lantern, with a richly profiled cornice and a softly curved hood bearing a spire and weathercock. The hood was also decorated with carved work full of volutes. However, the forms were not really modern but more like Renaissance features from the early 1600s. The lighthouse was rebuilt in 1699, but it vanished during a storm already in 1703.

During the 1580s, the French architect Louis de Foix made drawings for the lighthouse of Cordouan, at the mouth of the river Garonne. This combination of a beacon and chapel was finished in 1611, with a clear Renaissance style that suited the French state's lofty architectural image. The building resembles a spacious residence tower of a French castle, and its circular form was also the ideal one of the Renaissance. Pillars and pilasters hold up the first level of beams. Above these, colossal paired pilasters stretch up by two storeys, and the façade ends in a balustrade. Within the latter part is a chapel, whose cupola is visible in the outer roof. Over the domed roof is a smaller tower section, with pilasters between its round-arched windows. The uppermost part is a lantern for a wood fire, reached by a spiral staircase on the side.

Unfortunately, the lighthouse was rebuilt in the late 1700s and its upper part was torn down, replaced by a base for a higher tower section. This new section had a more cleanly functional structure in the spirit of Neoclassicism, very different from the surrounding Renaissance style. Nevertheless, from an architectural viewpoint, the building is still the most interesting lighthouse in the world.

In Sweden, all public construction during the 18th century was controlled by a state directorate. This was led by an architect, whose assignments could range from plain stone-arched bridges to castles and churches. Some beacons and lighthouses were also designed by these clever architects, whose drawings differ greatly from other, more amateurish proposals that reached the directorate. One of the most interesting, which was actually built, was the director Carl Hårleman's design of a lighthouse and its residence on Örskär in 1736. Hårleman drew a stone tower about 33 metres high, with a hexagonal lower part and a circular upper part, topped by an elegant wooden lantern with small leaded glass panes – all in well-balanced proportions. It was pretty and practical, but perhaps not very knowledgeable in regard to the care of the mirror beacons, since the beacon terrace was so narrow and had no railing. Or could the windows be opened inward for cleaning off snow, ice and dirt? Curious, too, is that there were no stairs: a smooth ramp went up to the watchroom for easier transport, especially of oil to the lamp apparatus.

In the 1770s, when the French government planned to build several new lighthouses at the mouth of the river Seine, it was decided to give them a representative design. The architect Pierre Penseron drew up three different proposals, which provide a good view of the changes in architectural style during this period. We can see both the late Baroque and the approaching Neoclassical forms of expression. None of the lighthouses were built according to these drawings, though, as it was then resolved to equip them with a more modern lighting technology.

The two lighthouses shown below at the left have richly decorated façades. They are mainly covered with rustic bands, typical at the time. One is divided into four storeys with decorative columns, segmented and triangular gables. The other is more tower-like, with manneristic colossal columns supporting a smaller fronton. The lighthouse below at the far right has been given a relatively modern, classicizing appearance: above the base storey, it resembles a large Tuscan column, all with smooth austere façades, decorated only with some classical sculptures.

The architect Pierre Penseron's plans from the 1770s for lighthouses at the mouth of the Seine.

A famous English architect, Decimus Burton, designed two lighthouses in the 1830s for the harbour of Fleetwood. They were strongly influenced by the style of Neoclassicism. The inner lighthouse, called Pharos, was given the form of a column with a base, standing on a square foundation of roughly cut stone. The lighthouse nearest to the sea had a square plan like a small temple, with Tuscan columns and pilasters that held up a balustraded terrace, on which the actual tower rested.

During the second half of the 18th century, there was a gradual transition from the stronger Baroque forms to a more pure classicism. In architecture, it was mainly columns that acquired a more definite function and were no longer only decorative elements. Architects who designed lighthouses found it easy to start with the classical column, especially the simple and severe Tuscan or Doric column. This proposal for a lighthouse at Ostende, Belgium in 1772 has the plain form of a Tuscan column, standing on a square base with a classicizing portal. The classical ideal can be no purer than this.

Another interesting example from England is the harbour light at Whitby, North Yorkshire. Designed by the engineer Francis Pickernell in 1831, it was almost a copy of a Doric column, with flutings and capital, standing on a base. The column supports the square terrace with a breast-wall and lantern.

The mixed styles of the 1800s

In the mid-19th century, the classicizing period gave way to what is called eclecticism or blending of styles. Architects could now borrow their means of expression from different earlier styles and even mix these in the same building. Together with new structural volumes, materials and methods, this resulted both in new variants of old styles and in completely novel, exciting façades. At the same time, architects felt free to use different styles for different types of buildings. A customer might have his edifice clothed in almost any architectural costume he wanted. Lighthouses were not connected with a special style, but display many distinctive forms.

The customary approach was to draw inspiration from medieval towers in combination with fortifications or churches. Thus a number of medieval-like lighthouses have Romanesque as well as Gothic features. One of the most magnificent lighthouses in such a neo-Gothic style was designed in the 1850s for Bremerhaven, by the German architect Simon Lochen.

Unlike the less orderly walls of French Gothicism, a fastidious Gothic use of bricks developed in northern Germany. Bricks were not as adaptable as natural stone, and simpler forms arose, such as blind windows and blind arches. The niches of blind windows in walls were often whitewashed, giving a nice contrast to the frequently red brick façade.

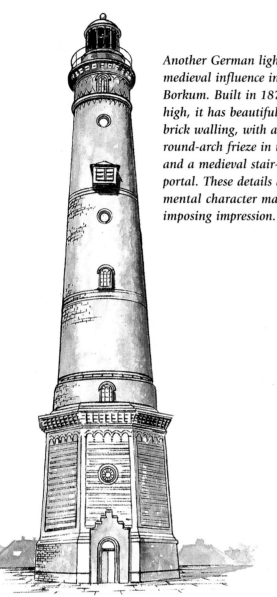

Another German lighthouse with medieval influence in its style is at Borkum. Built in 1879 and 60 metres high, it has beautifully patterned brick walling, with a Romanesque round-arch frieze in the high base and a medieval stair-gable over the portal. These details and its monumental character made a solid, imposing impression.

The lighthouse of Gross-Horst, Poland, was built in 1865-66 in a neo-Romanesque style, with well-marked round-arch windows, blind-arch friezes and corner-chains.

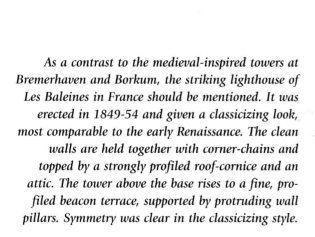

As a contrast to the medieval-inspired towers at Bremerhaven and Borkum, the striking lighthouse of Les Baleines in France should be mentioned. It was erected in 1849-54 and given a classicizing look, most comparable to the early Renaissance. The clean walls are held together with corner-chains and topped by a strongly profiled roof-cornice and an attic. The tower above the base rises to a fine, profiled beacon terrace, supported by protruding wall pillars. Symmetry was clear in the classicizing style.

Combined wooden lighthouse and residence buildings

The wooden lighthouses that were tried earlier in history usually came to a bad end. Their use of fire, and the effects of lightning, were often catastrophic. But the improvement of lamp technology in the 19th century, and the invention of lightning conductors, lessened the risk and made it possible to build safe wooden lighthouses. Steam-powered saws were now available to mass-produce boards at low prices, so that panel architecture in contemporary styles became ever more common. The lighthouse keepers' residences were frequently combined with a wooden lantern on the gable or roof. A house could also be inserted in a high framework tower of iron where the ground was porous, especially in the USA.

A combined lighthouse and residence made of wood, known as Fort Tompkins II in New Jersey, was built during the 1880s in a distinctive neo-Renaissance style. Richly decorated pilasters held up the roof-beams in both parts of the edifice. The high sloping roof crowned by elaborately carving was a feature often repeated in the late 19th century, and the clear chimneys gave an important impression of symmetry.

Engineering architecture

Techniques of iron production had been refined in the 1700s, rendering this material cheaper and easier to use for construction. Industrial progress was led by England, where the first iron bridge was built already in the 1770s, over the river Severn near Coalbrookdale. Such a novelty showed off the lightness, tension, transparency and delicacy that would become typical of many iron structures. The ultimate example was the French engineer Gustave Eiffel's iron tower, 300 metres high, at the World Exhibition in Paris in 1889.

But the buildings that we call engineering architecture were then regarded as utilities, having nothing to do with architecture. Iron was also at first considered hard to work with for artistic design. Therefore, it was normally covered up by more traditional materials in traditional styles. Still, by prefabricating their parts, buildings could be erected much faster and cheaper than before.

Iron and its technical applications were put to good use in erecting lighthouses during the 19th century. Cast, milled and forged iron were all employed – and here, too, England was a pioneer. An advantage of iron lighthouses was that they could be prefabricated in a workshop, transported to the site and set up rapidly, which was important since their locations were often dangerous and remote. Similarly, they could be dismantled and moved to another place if the need arose, and this was not unusual. Such lighthouses tended to cost less than conventional stone ones, although they rusted and called for constant maintenance.

Two different types of iron towers were developed. The first had a traditional form covered with sheet iron. The second was based on an invention of iron screw piles, which could be drilled into the ground to support a high framework. The latter type was especially suited on sandy ground, coral reefs and porous rocks, which had previously been impossible sites for lighthouses. And besides the above advantages, iron towers were unmatched for their ability to resist wind and waves, due to their open structure. With this design, engineers created several kinds of lighthouses from the 1830s onward, notably in England and America.

The lighthouse at Sand Key, off Florida, designed by George Meade and built in 1853.

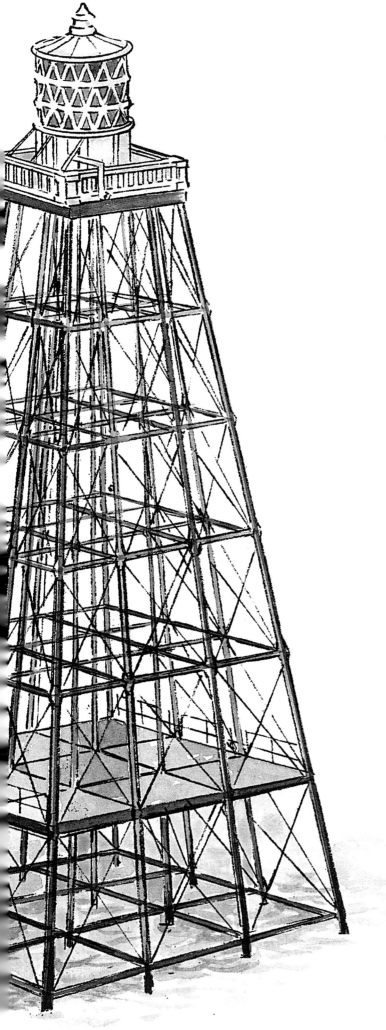

Scheveningen's lighthouse in Holland was built in the 1870s and covered by iron plates with bolted joints. Notice how the functional architecture is complemented with neo-Gothic features in the windows and portal. We recognize the typically Gothic pointed arch and the trefoil it encloses. Other artistic details are the usual corbels and railings of the beacon terrace.

The lighthouse of Kapell-udden on the island of Öland represents a model that was introduced to Sweden in the 1850s by the engineer of the pilotage administration, Nils Gustav von Heidenstam. Kapell-udden itself, built in 1872, was designed by the architect Albert Theodor Gellerstedt, who had a temporary job as a design assistant at the administration. He gave the lighthouse a portal with pilasters and beam level, a classicizing expression on an otherwise purely functional structure.

The lighthouse at Drum Point in the USA was built in 1883. Its lantern is placed centrally on the residence's roof. The beacon-house, with a peculiar cottage style, is supported by an iron structure that was screwed to the bottom where it stood. But it went out of use in 1962 and is now in the Calvert Maritime Museum, Maryland.

Concrete – the lighthouse material of the 20th century

Iron had revolutionized the construction of lighthouses, but it could not be used at its best until combined with concrete. In the modern sense, concrete was developed from Portland cement in the early 19th century. Concrete reinforced with iron provided enormous strength for durable structures, and thus became the main building material of the 1900s. Already during the 1870s it found many users in Great Britain, Germany and America. Well suited to various sorts of bridges, tunnels, towers, foundations and harbour works, concrete was also excellent for building lighthouses. All over the world, many concrete lighthouses appeared and the material gave them a more slender form.

The lighthouse of Understen in Sweden, about 40 metres high, was made of reinforced concrete. Designed by the engineer Folke Lundberg in 1915, it was erected a year by the pilotage administration's masterbuilder, Hilmer Carlsson. At this time, Swedish architects gladly clothed their façades in a national Romantic style, often with medieval inspiration. But the engineers were more practical and designed lighthouses mainly from a technical and functional viewpoint, as is well illustrated at Understen.

Subsequent developments during the 20th century led in different ways, with some interruptions, to the architecture known as modernism, which dominated the world by the 1940s. But classicizing forms were still used in lighthouses, for example the Faro della Vittoria at Trieste in Italy. This was built in 1923-27 and must be one of the century's most expensive lighthouses. A monument to drowned seamen, it was designed as a freely classical column with flutings on a strong base. The lantern is crowned by a bronze angel.

The lighthouse of Lågskär, off Åland (Finland), was designed by the Swedish construction company Kreuger & Toll. Built of concrete in 1919-20, it boasted an austere Egyptian obelisk, 33 metres high, with a classicizing entrance. Originally, though, the base storey was painted in a lighter hue.

Modernistic lighthouses

The breakthrough of modernism during the first half of the 20th century was the biggest change ever in architectural style. Its guiding star was function, which form had to follow. Previously well-decorated façades were replaced by bright, smooth walls, preferably with large glassed surfaces. The houses became simpler, with flat roofs. Function and structure were supposed to unite and be clearly visible. This radical new approach, however, had already been applied for a long time in lighthouses. When not designed by architects, the lighthouse was a purely technical utility with the most practical form possible, and then the engineer was the most suitable designer.

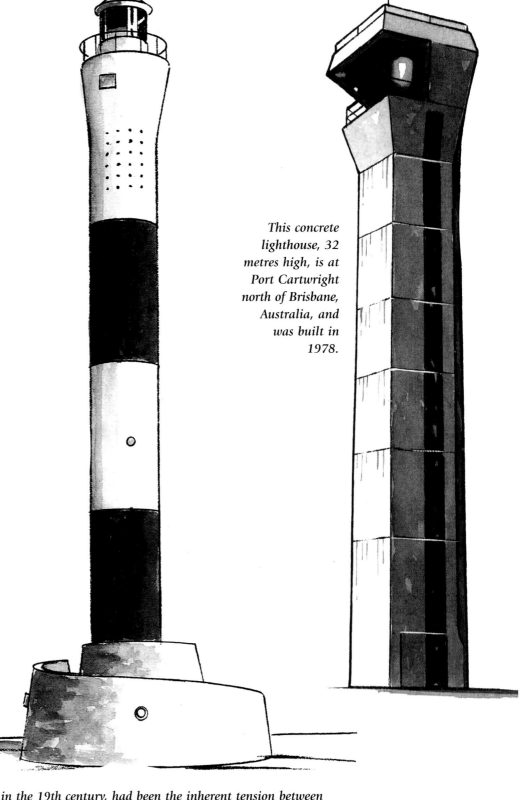

This concrete lighthouse, 32 metres high, is at Port Cartwright north of Brisbane, Australia, and was built in 1978.

Typical of lighthouse architecture, especially in the 19th century, had been the inherent tension between practicality and a desire for aesthetic appearance. This tension no longer existed in the stylistic ideal of modernism. Now the lighthouse as a technical structure was appreciated as one of the elemental, self-evident types of buildings by both engineers and architects.

The lighthouse at Dungeness in England, replacing an older one from 1904, was designed by Ronald Ward & Partners. Efficiently constructed from a series of concrete rings laid on top of each other, it was 40 metres high and took only six months to erect in 1961. Its robust foundation wall was essential for building in the loose sand. The lighthouse displays a modernistic, functional form that was typical of the time, and the section with a fog detector just under the lantern gives a decorative impression. Above this, the tower widens slightly and supports the terrace around the lantern.

The technique of building bottom-fixed lighthouses was developed by engineers, and resulted in new forms of beacons. It was a structural challenge to place and anchor lighthouses on sea or lake bottoms, and at first they were over-dimensioned for practical reasons. Once improved, they became slender and much more handsome, made of both concrete and iron. These carefully elaborated, cleverly constructed, functional buildings were eventually given the final modern touch of helicopter landing pads – which have also recently been added to older lighthouses. Shown here is the caisson lighthouse of Grundkallen, Sweden, designed by the engineer Robert Gellerstad and finished in 1959.

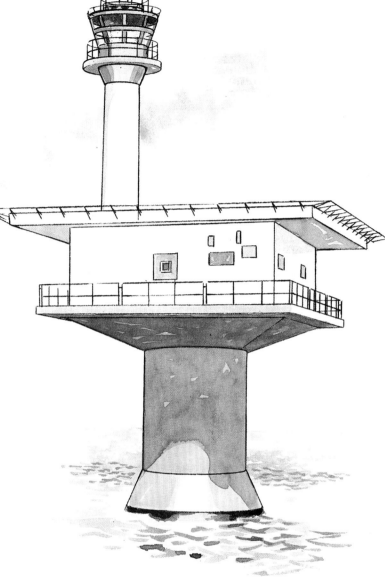

Another type of bottom-fixed lighthouse is the Canadian beacon platform of Pelee Passage, built in 1973.

The Coast Watchers in New Guinea was built as a beacon and monument in 1959. It might be seen as the product of a more sculptural approach to design. Note the stylized flame.

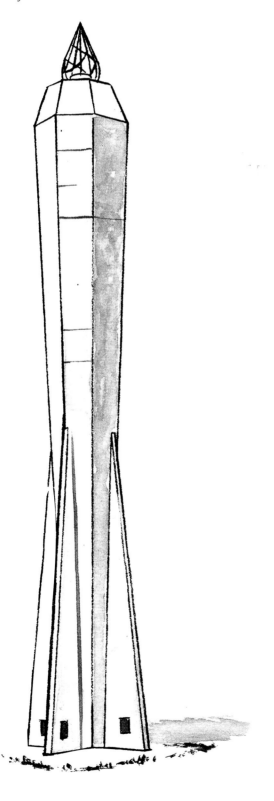

The lighthouse at Friedrichsort, Germany, is 33 metres high and was built in 1970. Its architecture can be compared directly to the lower tower from 1866.

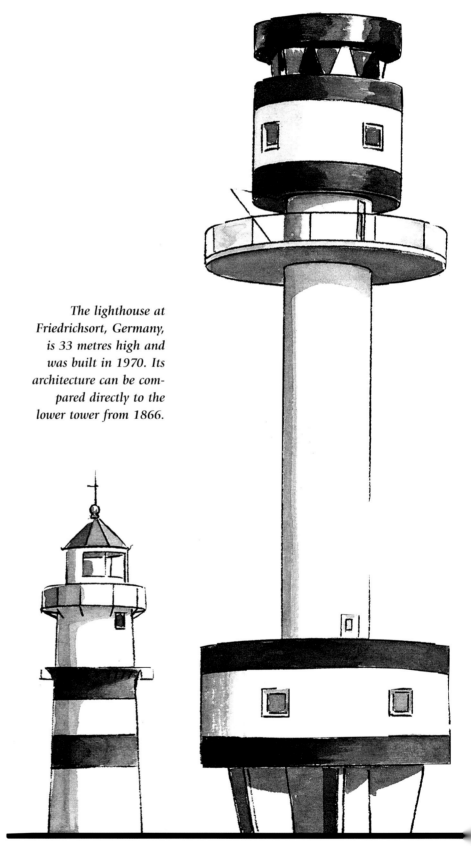

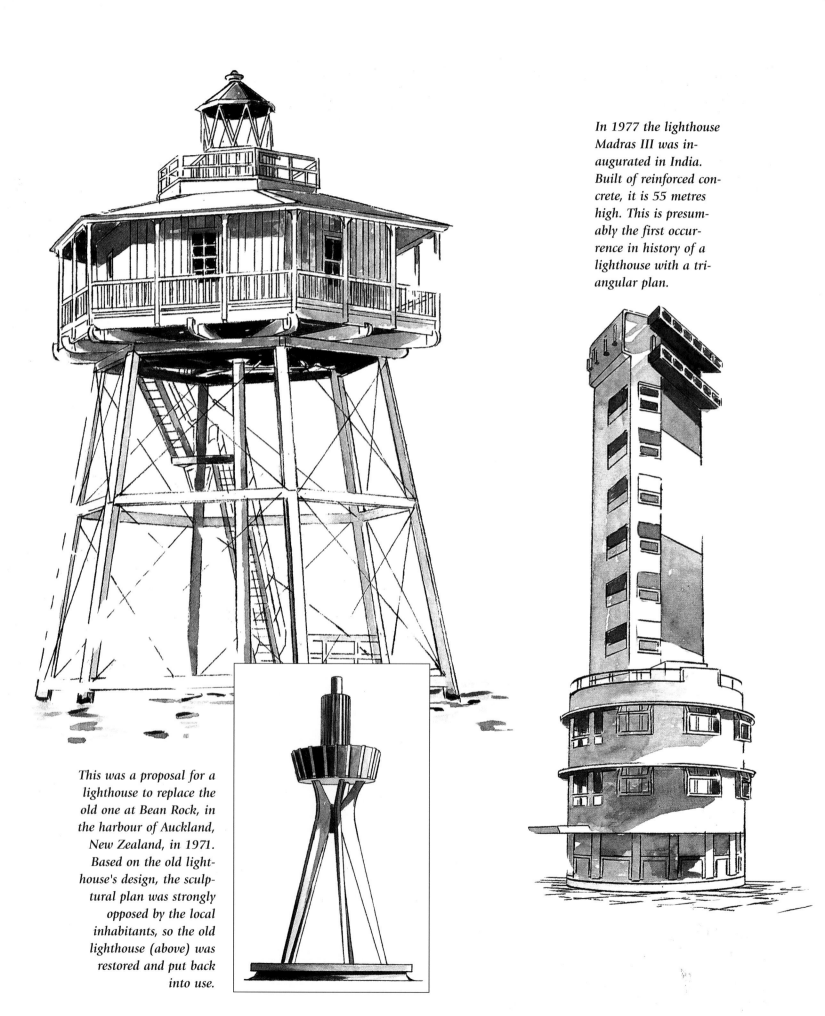

In 1977 the lighthouse Madras III was inaugurated in India. Built of reinforced concrete, it is 55 metres high. This is presumably the first occurrence in history of a lighthouse with a triangular plan.

This was a proposal for a lighthouse to replace the old one at Bean Rock, in the harbour of Auckland, New Zealand, in 1971. Based on the old lighthouse's design, the sculptural plan was strongly opposed by the local inhabitants, so the old lighthouse (above) was restored and put back into use.

Life at the Lighthouse

By the nature of their task, many lighthouses have to be established at places dangerous for seafaring – exposed environments that are quite unsuitable for building and living. Thus it has always been a challenge to erect these structures and residences, but to inhabit them has been the greatest challenge of all.

For a lighthouse to function, there was long a need of personnel who lit, maintained and extinguished the lights. To reduce the risk of a watchman falling asleep during the night shift, the work was divided into two or three periods, with a keeper who had the primary responsibility for the lighthouse.

The personnel's quarters either adjoined the lighthouse or lay nearby. Some lighthouses, especially those on small rocks in the sea or anchored on the ocean bottom, had residences within the lighthouse itself. Many of the locations were very isolated on islands, while others had a better position on the mainland. It was also usual for pilots to be stationed at lighthouses. Working and living conditions for the lighthouse families have varied widely.

The activities of the lighthouse personnel changed gradually with time. Those who served at wood and coal beacons endured the hardest labour. They had to cope with the fire under the open sky, until the early 1800s when it became possible to build an adequate lantern for this simple lighting technique. Things were often easier for the tenders of mirror or lens lights with glassed lanterns. But these required maintenance with greater care, and hence called for higher competence. Lenses and mirrors were polished, wicks were clipped, clockworks were opened and oiled. If faults occurred, an obvious advantage was to have technically adept personnel who could do repairs by themselves.

Common to all lighthouses, and particularly the tallest ones, was the heavy work of carrying up fuel to the lantern. It was frequently aided by different types of winch machinery, attached to the outside of the lighthouse. Below the lantern was normally the sparsely furnished watchroom.

Besides the lighthouse, many sites had equipment for fog signalling, which also belonged to the personnel's duties. The methods and instruments for warning seafarers in mist and thick fog have developed through the centuries. Bells, gongs, cannon shots, and blowing horns are among the oldest means. Towards the end of the 1800s, steam – and later, compressed air – came into use for powering foghorns, and then sirens. The resultant noise certainly helped those at sea, but was a plague to sleeping residents. At times, it could continue for several days and nights.

Well into the 19th century, there were still privately owned lighthouses, with personnel whose situation was largely governed by selfish motives of profit. The growth of ocean traffic, and of vessels bearing more valuable cargoes, led seafarers to place stronger demands on the state to take a principal responsibility for lighthouse administration. This eventually brought real improvements in both lighting technology and the care and maintenance of the lights – and thus safer sailing. The number of sites also increased considerably during the century.

At the isolated lighthouses, personnel were expected to have an extreme capacity for adapting to loneliness and their surroundings. This was still more true of their wives. The men had work to do with the lamps and caring for the buildings. In addition, they fished and hunted. Trips to land, for provisions and mail, were usually done by the men as well. Women, on the other hand, dealt with the household and children, and were therefore bound more closely to the site. The women also had to collaborate in the quarters for washing and baking, and sometimes even in those for cooking – which gave more reason for conflict. As everyone knew, the lighthouses where disagreement reigned were the hardest of all to live in. Further, with the increasing responsibility of central authorities for lighthouses and lighting technology, the personnel's level of competence was raised, leading to higher requirements for living standards and salaries.

Health care, and help in childbirth, were unthinkable at the isolated lighthouses. If possible, a pregnant woman might then be taken ashore in good time before the birth. However, trips to and from lighthouses have always been risky – especially before reliable weather reports could be issued and communicated to the site. The trips were made to transfer not only provisions and mail, but also children during the school terms. Many lighthouses, too, lay far up on rocks in the sea, causing a constant struggle to deliver materials and necessities.

To make matters worse, the harbour conditions were often very difficult at lighthouses. In wintertime, the sailing waters had freezing temperatures and their ice, both holding and breaking, was treacherous and rough to cross. As for schooling, in some countries where it was obligatory, temporary education was provided at sites with many children, and teachers lived at a number of lighthouses during certain seasons. Otherwise, the children were quartered on the mainland. The later 1900s, though, have brought helicopters to simplify such trips to lighthouses, many of which are equipped with landing pads.

The climate naturally played a great role in the families' conditions. At some light-houses, summer lasted almost all year round, while at others the long dreary winter meant total isolation from the outer world. For the latter, early spring was of special significance, but the personnel did all they could to enliven the rest of the year and make it as enjoyable as possible.

Considerable work was put into growing fruits and vegetables. Soil was transported to the site, and the farmland was shielded from the strong winds behind planks or walls. Many tried to plant bushes and trees, often with little success. Sheep, goats, or the occasional cow were frequently brought out if grazing was feasible.

An exciting diversion was to go round at times and see what floated ashore at the site. Life was not always so lonely and monotonous for the families at a lighthouse. Despite its warnings to seafarers, there remained the risk of nearby shipwrecks, drama and tragedy. Many heroic efforts were made to save lives, now and then rewarded with medals and distinctions. Not seldom, the personnel sheltered victims of a wreck for several days until the storm subsided. If they were able to help salvage cargo or other goods from the wreck, they could also earn a salvage fee. "The sea takes and the sea gives," it was said, and even the beaches were reputedly blessed by numerous priests.

Regardless of the very peculiar circumstances at lighthouses, their profession was commonly passed down from generation to generation. Its enthusiasts were often people who had been born on the coasts – or had previously spent years as seamen, which in some countries was one of the basic requirements for employment.

The ultimate aim was to obtain a post as a keeper, the highest office at a lighthouse. Such a job paid better, and led to a better pension. But to advance so far, a lighthouse family might well need to change its location several times.

For some individuals, the solitude at these sites became unbearable and they turned to other occupations. Having a family tended to be a strength and a prerequisite for tolerating this kind of environment. An isolated lighthouse rarely had visitors – although there was one which caused a degree of nervousness. The owner, usually a representative of the state, arrived at intervals to inspect the site's buildings, technical equipment and inventories.

Among the most memorable events in their lives, according to many of the older families, was when radio reached the lighthouses. Today, it may be hard for us to understand the feeling that filled their hearts at the sound of voices from the mainland, including the services in churches. Similarly, lighthouses that acquired telephones were never the same again.

The 20th century has brought a slow end to the era of lighthouse residents. Progress in lighting technology made them ever less essential, and sites around the world have been ever less manned since the 1960s. At some places, this is delayed by the personnel's adoption of other tasks such as weather observation and marine surveillance. Still, complete disappearance is in store for manned lighthouses – a prominent feature in the history of seafaring. Recent years have also allowed satellite navigation to justify turning out their lights, and even threatening them with demolition.

Lighthouses around the world

There are many thousands of lighthouses throughout the world. Some are short and relatively dim, while others are tall and equipped with a strong light that is visible far and wide. All lighthouses, however, have been built according to specific needs and are adapted to the conditions that seafarers in all ages have been forced to obey.

The closer to land a vessel has come, the more important it has been to navigate correctly so as, for example, to avoid running aground. Regardless of when a lighthouse was built, where it stands and how it is designed, its aim has always been the same: to aid and create conditions for navigating by dark.

As seafaring developed and the numbers of ships increased, the demand for lighthouses became ever greater. Most lighthouses are comparatively small and lie near harbours and ports, but there are also many out at sea which have the task of leading sea traffic in toward land. This diversity of lighthouses, and their frequent location in exposed – as well as exciting – places, lends a natural fascination to such "lights in the dark". For a long time, lighthouses have been a necessity for sailors; yet in addition, they are a part of our cultural history and these powerful buildings will continue to set our imaginations in motion, even though their practical significance for merchant traffic at sea has declined to a minimum today.

Types of lights

Whatever its size and bright-ness, a beacon or lighthouse has the primary purpose of warning ships about shallow water, showing the way in, and helping to establish a vessel's position. Light buoys, spar buoys and lightships are also considered to be beacons. Fishing lights, too, exist which are specially adapted to pro-fessional fishermen and thus often have a limited range of visibility.

Several types of lights can be distinguished, but they are usually grouped as approach lights and leading lights. The former, also called coastal lights, are high – or placed high up – with very strong illumination, and often lie in the outer archipelago. Leading lights are meant to lead ves-sels properly in fairways, en-trances to archipelagos, and harbour inlets, for example. A third group contains what are known as warning lights.

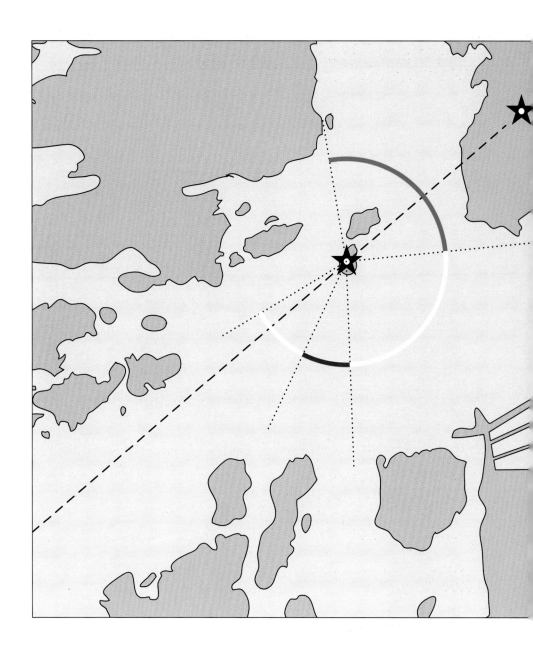

Lightships are frequently located far from land to help vessels navigate out to sea. There are also lightships that serve as approach points at entrances, but lightships have also been placed in narrow channels to serve the same purpose as leading lights. As a rule, lightships are painted red, with the light station's name in white letters on both the port and starboard sides. Due to serious operational problems, however, most lightships have been replaced by large bottom-fixed beacons.

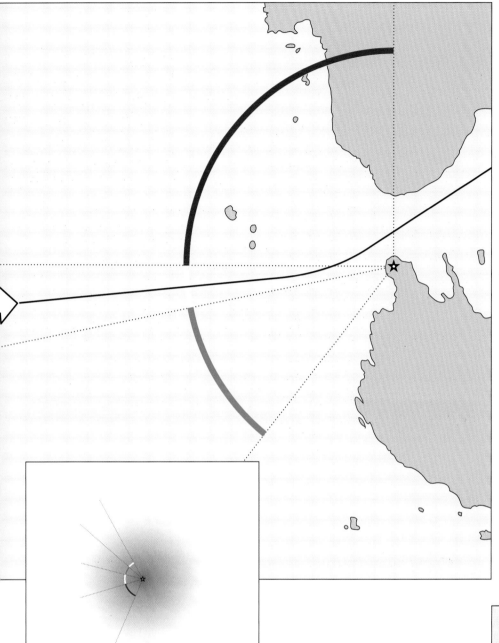

Leading lights are weaker than approach lights and have a shorter range. They are normally divided into lights in line and sector lights. Lights in line always lie in pairs and mark out a straight fairway if they agree, that is, form a straight line – and the nearer light is usually placed lower than the farther one. Sector lights generally shine white, green and red in particular directions. The white light shows that the ship is in the fairway and can proceed without risk, while the green and red lights indicate that it is outside the fairway on the port or starboard side, respectively.

Since lightships tended to lie over deep water far from land, so-called caisson lights were built to replace them. The world's first caisson light arose in 1885 at Rothersand outside Bremerhaven. The advantages of a caisson light were that it needed fewer personnel than a lightship, it stood firmly on the bottom even in great depths of water, and was relatively cheap to operate and maintain. The light's lower part was constructed at a quay or on land, and towed out to be sunk in position. Once it was well anchored, the upper building was added. The "telescope method", invented by Robert Gellerstad in Sweden, even enabled the whole light to be built on land before it was towed out, when its inner section – the telescope – was raised to the correct height and connected to electricity.

Light characters

The ability to distinguish lights from each other in the dark, and thereby identify them, is necessary in order to navigate by them and determine a ship's position. As a result, very few beacons nowadays shine without any variation. To make them distinct, the lights show regular changes in brightness which are called characters. Some beacons send out several light signs in a group, whose length of time – from the first sign's beginning until this is seen again – is known as a period. The character of a light is always measured in seconds.

The type of beacon may thus be either a fixed light, an isophase light (with equal intervals of brightness and darkness), a flashing light (for at most 0.7 seconds), a long-flashing light (for at least 2 seconds), or an occulting light (with longer bright than dark intervals). On sea charts, the character of a light is shown by a symbol such as Fl (fixed), Q (quick continuous flashing), LFl (long-flashing) or Iso (isophase).

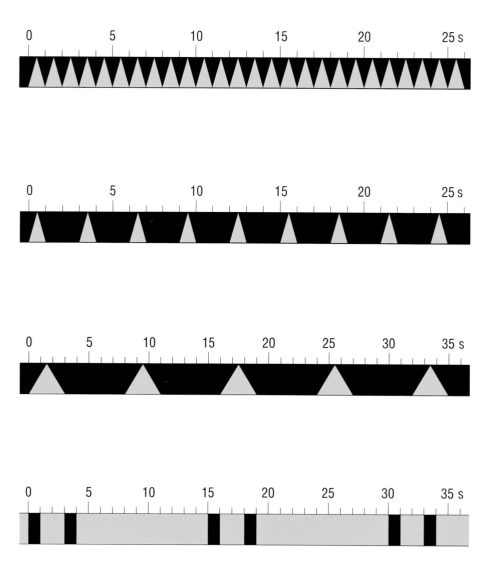

Some examples of light characters and their designations are illustrated here.

Sea charts indicate most of the important information about a light, for instance its position, colour, period, direction angles, range, and sometimes even its height above the water and how its building looks. The main details for identifying a light in the dark are its character, colours and period. Besides the symbol for its character, the colours may be shown as W (white), R (red) and G (green), but are not indicated if the light only shines white. The period, given in seconds, shows the duration between each group of signals and the next group.

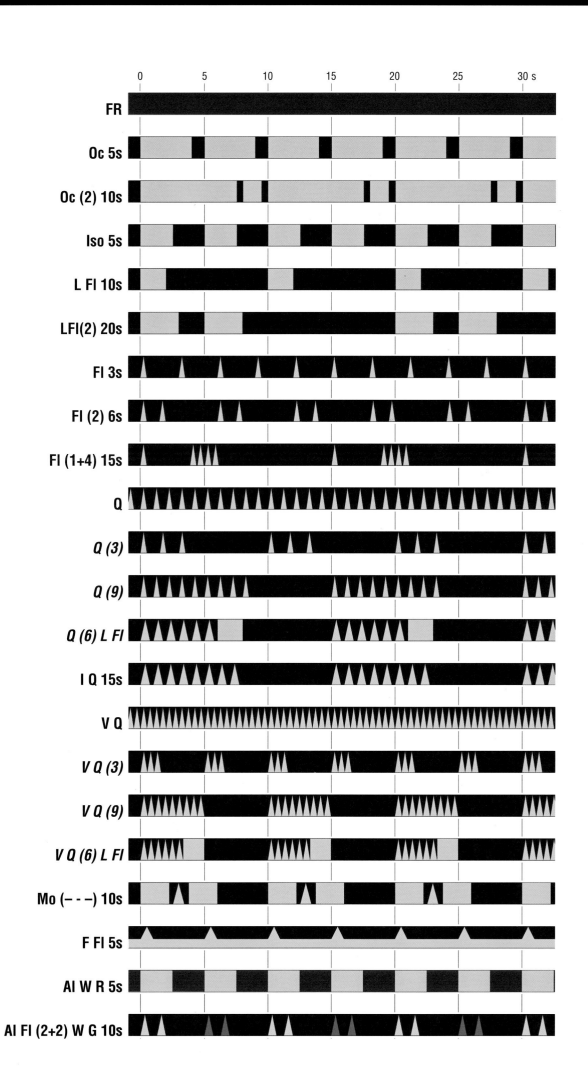

On following pages are some of the world´s largest coastal lighthouses indicated. Most of them have more than 20 nautical miles in range of visibility and are used for determining position when approaching coasts. Many are provided with mist-signal senders that can be heard in fog. A lot of them also have a radar beacon, which activates when hit by the ship´s radar emission and then can be seen on the radar screen.

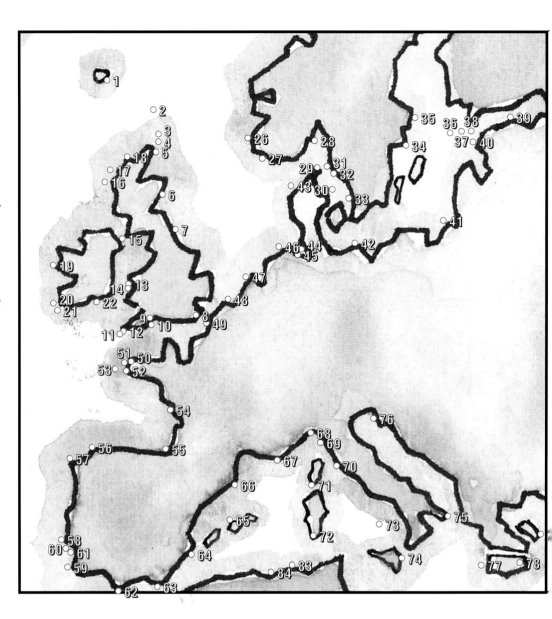

1.	Dyrholaey	23.	Cape Stolbiovo	45.	Bremerhaven	67.	Cape Camarat
2.	Myggenaes	24.	Kharlov Island	46.	Helgoland	68.	Punta del Faro
3	Sumburgh Head, Shetland Islands	25.	Vardöy	47.	Terschelling Brandaris	69.	La Lanterna, Genova
4	Muckle Flugga	26.	Udsira	48.	Hook of Schouwen	70.	Livorno
5	Dunnet Head	27.	Lista	49.	Cape Gris-Nez	71.	Cape Pertusato
6	Bell Rock	28.	Færder	50.	Ile Vierge	72.	Cape Sandalo
7.	Whitby	29.	Skagen	51.	Le Stiff	73.	Imperatore Point, Ischia
8.	South Foreland	30.	Anholt	52.	La Jument	74.	Milazzo
9.	Needles Point	31.	Vinga	53.	Ouessant	75.	Cape Santa Maria di Leuca
10.	Eddystone	32.	Nidingen	54.	Courdouan	76.	Savudrija
11.	Bishop Rock	33.	Kullen	55.	Biarritz	77.	Sapientza
12.	Lizard	34.	Landsort	56.	Hercules Tower, La Coruna	78.	Parapola
13.	Skerries Rock	35.	Grundkallen	57.	Cape Finisterre	79.	Cape Armenisti
14.	The Smalls	36.	Bogskär	58.	Cape Roca	80.	Cape Meganom
15.	Mull of Galloway	37.	Utö	59.	Cape St.Vincent	81.	Mount Carmel
16.	Barra Head	38.	Bengtskär	60.	Guia	82.	Cape Carthage
17.	Flannan Islands, Hebrides	39.	Hogland	61.	Bugio	83.	Cape de Garde
18.	Cape Wrath	40.	Kopu, Dager Ort	62.	Europe Point	84.	Cape Carbon
19.	Blackrock Mayo	41.	Rozawie	63.	Mesa de Roldán	85.	Ceuta
20.	Bull Rock	42.	Arkona	64.	Cape Nao	86.	Cape Spartel
21.	Fastnet Rock	43.	Hirtshals	65.	Porto Pi, Mallorca	87.	Ribeirinha Point, Fayal
22.	Hook Head	44.	Neuwerk	66.	Cape San Sebastian	88.	Ferraria Point, San Miquel

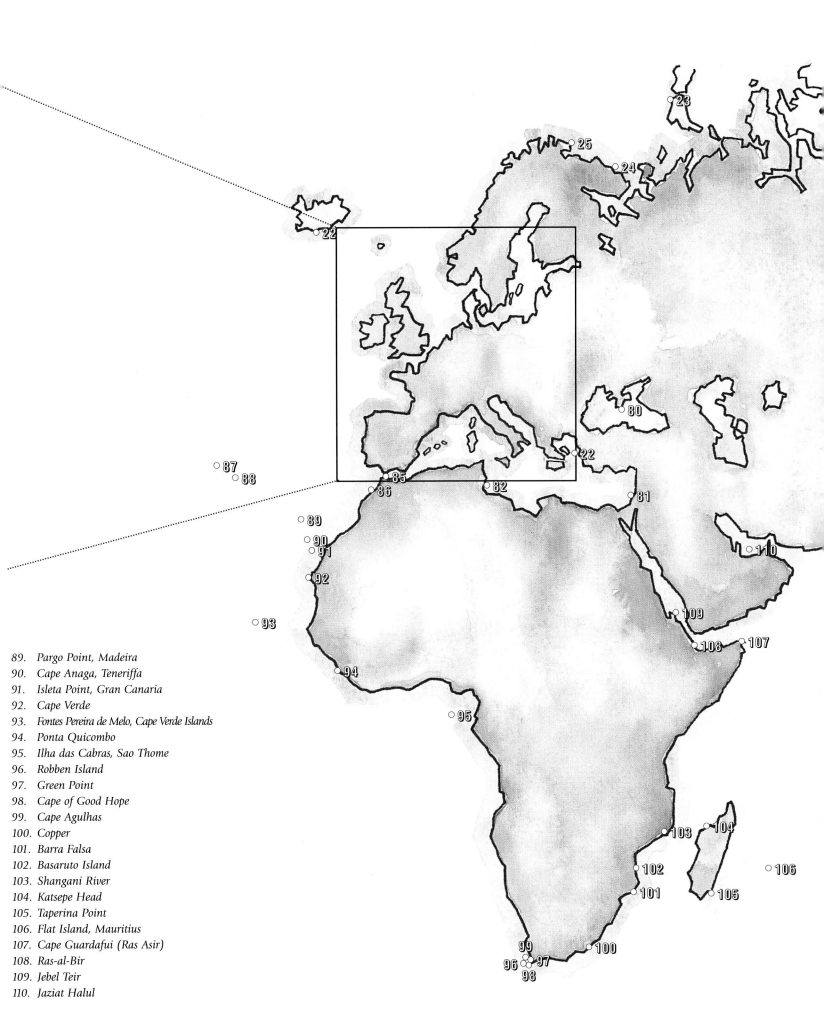

89. Pargo Point, Madeira
90. Cape Anaga, Teneriffa
91. Isleta Point, Gran Canaria
92. Cape Verde
93. Fontes Pereira de Melo, Cape Verde Islands
94. Ponta Quicombo
95. Ilha das Cabras, Sao Thome
96. Robben Island
97. Green Point
98. Cape of Good Hope
99. Cape Agulhas
100. Copper
101. Barra Falsa
102. Basaruto Island
103. Shangani River
104. Katsepe Head
105. Taperina Point
106. Flat Island, Mauritius
107. Cape Guardafui (Ras Asir)
108. Ras-al-Bir
109. Jebel Teir
110. Jaziat Halul

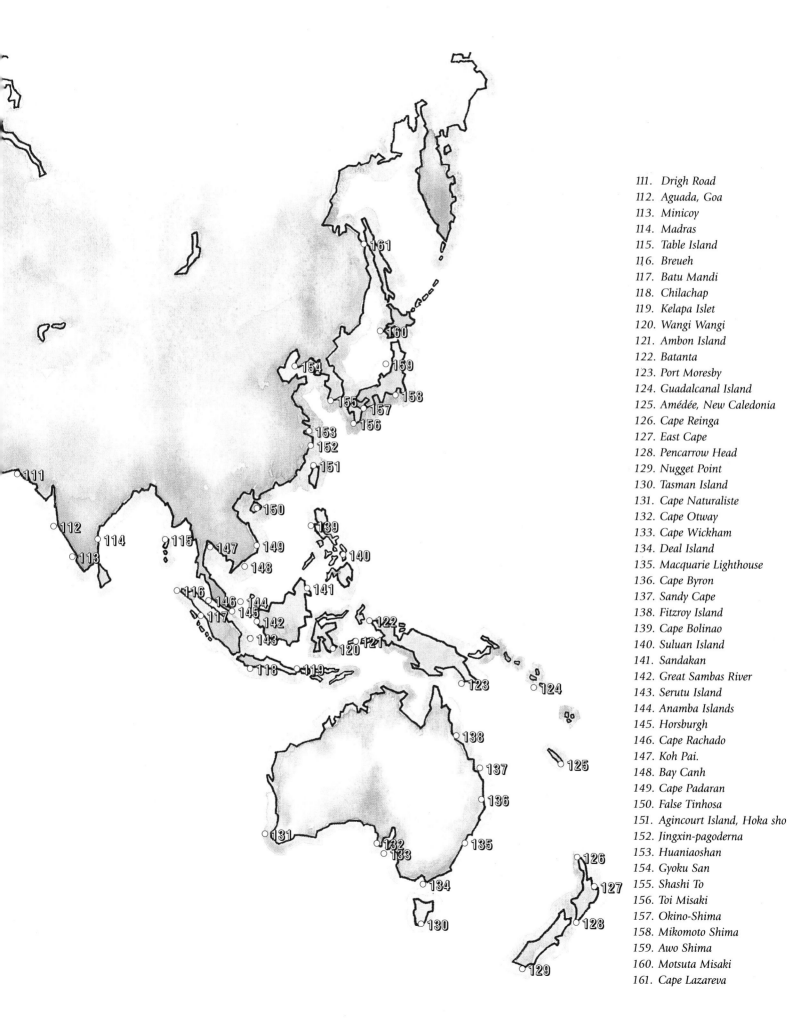

111. Drigh Road
112. Aguada, Goa
113. Minicoy
114. Madras
115. Table Island
116. Breueh
117. Batu Mandi
118. Chilachap
119. Kelapa Islet
120. Wangi Wangi
121. Ambon Island
122. Batanta
123. Port Moresby
124. Guadalcanal Island
125. Amédée, New Caledonia
126. Cape Reinga
127. East Cape
128. Pencarrow Head
129. Nugget Point
130. Tasman Island
131. Cape Naturaliste
132. Cape Otway
133. Cape Wickham
134. Deal Island
135. Macquarie Lighthouse
136. Cape Byron
137. Sandy Cape
138. Fitzroy Island
139. Cape Bolinao
140. Suluan Island
141. Sandakan
142. Great Sambas River
143. Serutu Island
144. Anamba Islands
145. Horsburgh
146. Cape Rachado
147. Koh Pai.
148. Bay Canh
149. Cape Padaran
150. False Tinhosa
151. Agincourt Island, Hoka sho
152. Jingxin-pagoderna
153. Huaniaoshan
154. Gyoku San
155. Shashi To
156. Toi Misaki
157. Okino-Shima
158. Mikomoto Shima
159. Awo Shima
160. Motsuta Misaki
161. Cape Lazareva

162. *Makapuu Point, Oahu*
163. *Molokai*
164. *Cape Hinchinbrook*
165. *Cape St. James,*
    Queen Charlotte Island
166. *Main Channel*
167. *Cape Blanco*
168. *Cape Mendocino*
169. *Farallon, San Francisco*
170. *Point Sur*
171. *Anacapa Island*
172. *West Benito Island*
173. *Natividad Island*
174. *Cape Tosco*
175. *Guaymas, Cape Haro*
176. *Cerro Partido*
177. *Mazatlán*
178. *Punta de Campos*
179. *Acapulco, Grifo Island*
180. *Golfito*
181. *Santa Elena Point*
182. *Callao*
183. *Atico Point*
184. *Curaumilla Point*
185. *Guafo Island*
186. *New Year's Islands,*
    Staten Island
187. *Cape Virgins*
188. *Leones Isle*

189. *Colonia del Sacramento*
190. *Arvoredo Islet*
191. *Castelhanos Point*
192. *Cape Frio*
193. *Santo Antonio*
194. *Cape Agostinho*
195. *Mel Point*
196. *Chacachacare Islet, Trinidad*
197. *El Roque*
198. *Cartagena*
199. *Manzanillo Point*
200. *Bocas del Toro*
201. *Port Cortez*
202. *Roca Partida*
203. *La Trinité Bay, Martinique*
204. *Hams Bluff, St. Croix*
205. *Cape Borinquén*
206. *Guantánamo*
207. *Castillo del Morro*
208. *Pensacola*
209. *Cape Florida Light*
210. *St. Augustine*
211. *Gibb's Hill, Bermuda*
212. *Cape Hatteras*
213. *Chapel Hill Beacon*
214. *Staten Island*
215. *Cape Cod*
216. *Boston Harbour Light*
217. *Sambro Island*
218. *Cape Gaspé*
219. *Cape Pine*
220. *Belle Isle*

Eddystone (England)

In the 17th and 18th centuries, a heyday of sailing vessels, the city of Plymouth on England's south coast was an important, and safe, harbour for the ships going to and from the New World. The harbour was also a very essential port for the fleet in all naval battles against France and Spain. Yet an approach to the harbour by night was worrying, because about 14 miles south of the entrance lay a large, terrifying reef of stone. The reef could only be seen at low water and, for decades, thousands of ships had sunk there with their crews and cargoes. The need to mark the reef was obvious, but Trinity House – the English lighthouse administration – considered it too risky, and indeed impossible, to build a beacon on a rock in the midst of the sea.

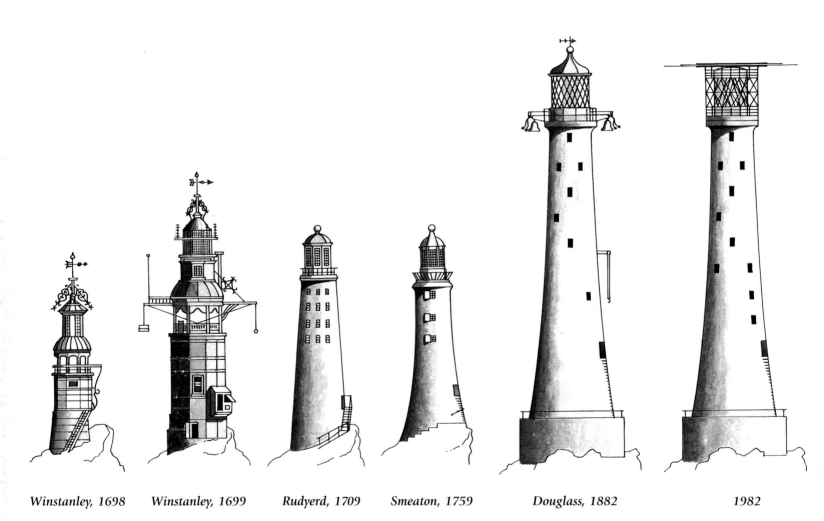

Winstanley, 1698   Winstanley, 1699   Rudyerd, 1709   Smeaton, 1759   Douglass, 1882   1982

Henry Winstanley, a shipowner with diverse interests, had two vessels and one of them sank on the rocks outside Plymouth at the end of the 1600s. He demanded that the authorities build a beacon on these rocks, but was told that nobody could be found who was able to carry out such a task. This highly impulsive man replied that he himself was able, and would set up a beacon on Eddystone.

What resulted was the world's first beacon to be built on a water-washed rock in the ocean. Construction began in 1696, when Winstanley turned 51, and was finished in the autumn of 1698 after three years of labour. During much of the time, this rock was inundated by waves and tides, so the work was extremely dangerous. In those days, moreover, there were no building engineers or others with experience of masonry and casting under water. In the first summer season, it was only possible to bore 12 holes in the sloping rock surface, and to fasten iron rods in them. In the winter, stone blocks were quarried and shaped on land, to be freighted out during the next summer, one by one, and attached with some type of cement to the rock surface between the iron rods.

England was then at war with France, and all the workers on the beacon were captured by the French navy and taken to France. But they were immediately released by King Louis XIV, who apologized and explained that he was fighting England – not individuals. After their return to England, the work continued, and this second summer saw the successful construction of a tower, 3.7 metres high and 4.3 metres in diameter. Next year, the base was enlarged to a height of 5.5 and diameter of 4.9 metres. On top of this, the lighthouse was built with residence quarters and a lantern.

The light was first lit on November 14, 1698, with tallow lamps tended by three men. They had an awful winter, as the lighthouse was constantly shaken by storms and pounded by the sea. Next summer, it was therefore heightened by 7 metres and the base diameter increased to 7.4 metres. Then, too, it was decorated with much ironwork and various lifting cranes. Meanwhile, no shipwrecks had occurred on the Eddystone rocks, and the beacon was definitely regarded as one of the world's wonders.

As the lighthouse still shook during storms, Winstanley decided to live there himself for some nights and study the problem in detail. On the night of November 25/26, 1703, England was struck by one of the worst storms ever – and the next morning, both the Eddystone beacon and Winstanley, as well as all the personnel, were gone. The following day, the first ship in five years foundered on the Eddystone rocks!

It was now realized that a beacon on Eddystone was indispensable, and a silk merchant from Cornwall named John Rudyerd was appointed to build a new one. He had no experience of building, but was clever enough to think that a lighthouse should be like a ship, so he employed some carpenters. They decided that the edifice should be covered externally with planks which were tarred like a boat. Inside, there would be a mast to keep the lighthouse stable, yet also flexible. As much weight as possible would be placed at the base to provide ballast.

The construction began in the summer of 1706 and was finished in the autumn of 1708. No decorations or projecting parts were on the lighthouse, so that waves could easily pass by it. Steps were cut out of the sloping rock, and iron rods were fastened with lead in 36 bored holes. With the help of oak blocks, the rock was made

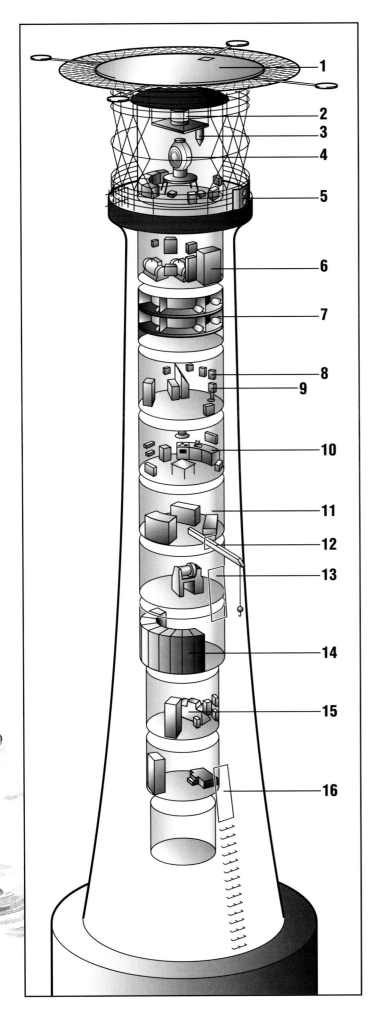

horizontal, and then alternating layers of stone and oak were laid up to the levels of the residence and the light. The beacon stood securely and spread its glow for many years. However, there was trouble with woodworms in the outer planking – another reminder of boats.

On December 1, 1755, the watch from midnight to 4 AM was taken by Henry Hall, aged 94. He discovered that a fire had started in the soot and tallow inside the lantern, and was spreading to the outer planks. The personnel hid in a rock crevice and the lighthouse burned down. But the weather was good and, in the morning, a boat sailed out to rescue the frightened watchmen. The violent fire had also melted the lantern's lead roof. When Henry Hall later reported that he had swallowed a piece of melted lead that fell down, no one believed him. Yet he died 12 days later, and the autopsy revealed a large lump of lead in his stomach!

Now the third lighthouse at Eddystone was gone, and another had to be built as soon as possible. This time, the task went to John Smeaton, an engineer and mathematician. He began the work in August 1756, and the light was lit in October 1759. Before starting, he made careful measurements at the site, and beveled out the rock so that stone blocks could be attached with zinc. Each stone layer resembled a puzzle, also linked together with rods of marble and wood. Smeaton thought that the lighthouse should rise out of the rock like a branch from a tree. There would be no projecting parts, and a bulge below the lantern would deflect the waves outward from it. Thus, the first modern offshore lighthouse was created, and the same design is still used today. Smeaton also developed a cement that hardened in water.

His lighthouse functioned excellently and no further shipwrecks occurred. It became legendary and was portrayed on English copper pennies of certain years. While it survived all of nature's attacks, the waves began to undermine the cliff where it stood. Thus, a new lighthouse next to it was designed and built by James N. Douglass. This one began to operate in 1882 and is still used today. Smeaton's old light was then extinguished and his lighthouse was dismanted, stone by stone, to be reconstructed on a summit in Plymouth – where it now stands looking out at its replacement on the Eddystone rocks.

1.	Helipad	10.	Kitchen (for visiting officials)
2.	Emergency light		
3.	Racon	11.	Batteries and storage
4.	Main light	12.	Jib
5.	Fog signal	13.	Winch room (sea landings)
6.	Upper engine room		
7.	Bedroom (for visiting officials)	14.	Fuel storage
		15.	Lower engine room
8.	Battery chargers and radio link	16.	Lower entrance (sea landings)
9.	Subsidiary light		

Bishop Rock (England)

Located on rocks in the sea off the Scilly Isles in the Atlantic, Bishop Rock is the first English lighthouse seen by ships approaching from the west. Countless vessels through the centuries have foundered on these rocks – including the British Navy's 50-cannon frigate HMS Romney which, in October 1707, was wrecked with 400 men. In the mid-1800s, the number of wrecks had reached epidemic proportions and the Trinity House administration decided that a lighthouse had to be built on Bishop Rock.

Bishop Rock I (1847-50)   Bishop Rock II (1852-87)   Bishop Rock III (1887-)

Work began in the summer of 1848 by boring holes in the rocks. Then it took two years to erect an iron tower, in which the light would be mounted. But all this, and the cost of £12,500, were lost in a storm on February 5, 1850, which also destroyed many houses in the Scilly Isles.

Due to the great need for a lighthouse here, the work was resumed on what would now be a stone beacon. The perilous project continued for seven years, and finally the 33.5-metre-high tower was lit up on September 1, 1858. Once it was completed, Prince Albert proclaimed in a speech that Bishop Rock was a triumph of engineering and tenacity. The cost of the building came to £36,599.

During a storm on April 20, 1874, waves over 35 metres high pounded the lighthouse, and its keepers expected to die. Next summer, therefore, it was strengthened, but a storm in the winter of 1881 broke heavy pieces of granite from it. As it was no longer considered safe, a new lighthouse was planned. The builder was the man who constructed the contemporary lighthouse of Eddystone. Work began at Bishop Rock in 1883 and the new light was first lit on October 25, 1887. This lighthouse cost £64,889 and is still standing.

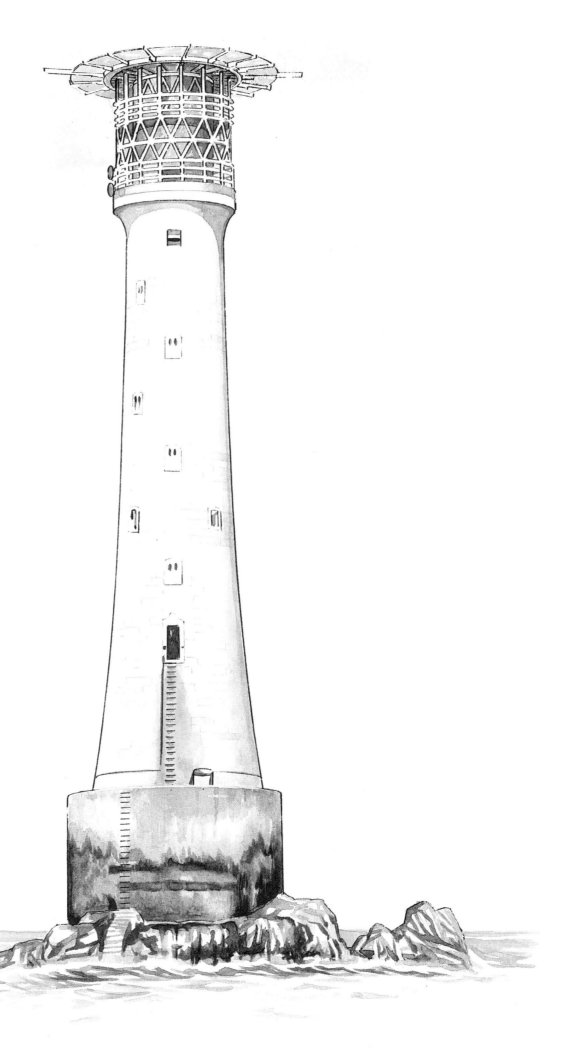

Skerries Rock
(England)

In England, many lighthouses were originally in private owner-ship, despite the existence of the Trinity House administration since the 1500s. The owner paid for building a beacon, bought the right to operate it by paying a licence fee to Trinity House, and collected fees from passing ships. Trinity House did not need to invest in lighthouses, but granted permits to erect them.

Owning lighthouses gradually became very profitable, and Trinity House began to buy them all back for large sums of money. Skerries Rock was the last privately owned light-house in England, and the most expensive when, in 1841, Trinity House bought it for £444,984. Even this high price was earned back by the administration as soon as 1850.

The lighthouse of Skerries Rock stands on a reef outside the ferry harbour of Holyhead in Wales. A beacon at this dangerous place had been wanted since the mid-1600s, but not until 1710 did Trinity House give permission to build one. In 1716 the work commenced on a light-house 11 metres high, and it was first lit on November 4, 1717. All the shipowners and others who had desired it, however, now did their best to avoid paying the beacon fees, so the owner died poor.

This lighthouse was torn down in 1759 and replaced by one with a coal fire in an iron basket. Trinity House decided in 1777 that Skerries Rock was one of the two worst-man-aged beacons in England. The next year, there-fore, it received a new owner who ensured that it was tended perfectly for the following 26 years. In 1803 it was restored and given new lighting, with 16 Argand lamps and reflectors. Trinity House later acquired it, and in 1844 it was raised and modernized again. The "new" light was lit in September 1846.

The Smalls
(England)

Twenty nautical miles off the southwest cape of Wales, in the midst of all main fairways passing that region, lies the Smalls reef. It protrudes only about 4 metres above the sea at normal water levels. Many ships once ran aground there, and discussions long took place on how to make the passage safer. In 1773 the reef was rented by an individual who intended to build a beacon and collect fees. He hired a maker of musical instruments to do the design and construction.

Originally the beacon was to be erected on an iron framework anchored in the rock. Breaking waves would thus flow through the framework, under the lighthouse itself. But the design was revised before the work began, and the iron rods were exchanged for strong oak piles. The building was constructed on the mainland, then taken apart, shipped out to the reef and reassembled. After much difficulty, the light was kindled in 1777. This design, with a lighthouse supported by several wooden piles, later became very popular all over the world. The Smalls lighthouse also earned plenty of profit for its owner. In 1861 it was replaced by the present tower of granite, 42 metres high.

Needles Point
(England)

The Isle of Wight lies shielding the important English maritime cities of Southampton and Portsmouth. Between it and them is a sizeable area of ocean, the Solent. When sailing into the Solent from the west, one has the lighthouse of Needles Point to starboard. Like most other English lighthouses, it stands at a quite exposed place – on a reef projecting from the Isle of Wight. The first beacon built at the entrance to the Solent, in 1787, was located far up on the island above the entrance, but went out of use after some years, being usually hidden in fog.

Seafaring grew enormously during the Victorian era, resulting in a decision to build a new lighthouse here. This was 49 metres high and went into operation on May 22, 1859; it is still shining today. However, its location not only meant great exposure to wind and waves. Another danger, for the personnel, arose in World War II when German airplane pilots used the lighthouse regularly as a practice target. Innumerable glass panes in the lantern were shot out during the war, although luckily the tower was never hit by bombs. Throughout the war, the lighthouse keepers found shelter in a storeroom dug into the limestone rocks.

Bell Rock
(Scotland)

Bell, or Inchape, Rock lies outside the city of Arbroath on the east coast of Scotland. According to tradition, the rock got its name from a bell which a monk set up on the rock during the 1300s to warn seafarers. Later, the bell was reputedly stolen by a Dutch pirate, who subsequently ran aground and drowned on the rock.

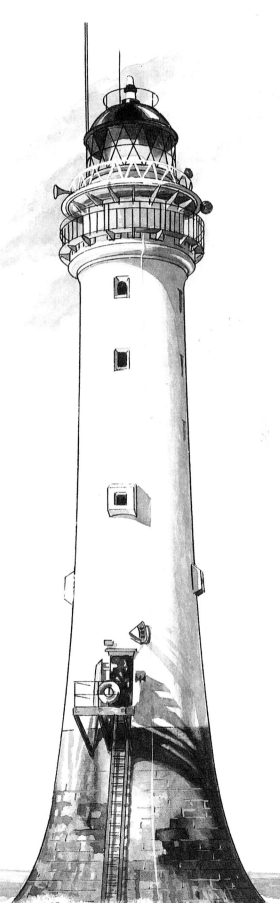

Many ships were wrecked at the place, but it was considered impossible to construct a beacon, since the rock was at least as exposed to weather and wind as Eddystone and Bishop Rock. Besides, it was mostly covered by water. In the early 1800s, the feat was accomplished of setting up three wooden beacons, yet they disappeared as soon as they were lit. The only alternative was to try building a lighthouse, and this became the second occulting light in the world, after Eddystone.

The nearly impossible task of erecting the lighthouse was given to a Scottish beacon engineer, Robert Stevenson (1772-1850). He was to be followed by five

more generations of lighthouse builders in his family. Another of his relatives was the author Robert Louis Stevenson.

Robert Stevenson was an unusually clever, thoughtful and also religious man. In 1807 he began to employ smiths, stone-cutters, carpenters and foremen. To transport men and materials to the rock, two sailboats were acquired. These were named Pharos and Smeaton (see the description of Eddystone Rock). The Pharos was later anchored at the rock and used as overnight quarters near the building site, so that working time was not lost by travelling to and from land.

During the autumn of 1807, a residence began to be built on piles, 15 metres above the rock, so that the men could live on the rock while working. In October, this work stopped and they started to cut stone blocks on the mainland for the next season. The very hard labour continued with preparations on land during the winter, and the rest of the year was spent on the rock.

At times, those who lived in the barracks on the reef thought that they would be swept into the water. On a couple of occasions, the waves even broke windows and parts of the walls in the barracks. Each Sunday the residents attended a church service, normally conducted by Stevenson who lived there as well.

On February 1, 1811, the light was first lit. Stevenson and his men had built a masterpiece, rising 115 feet above the sea. It contains 28,350 cubic feet of stone, weighing 2,076 tons, and cost £61,331. The lighthouse has gradually been modernized, but it stands as beautiful and impressive today as when it was inaugurated.

Muckle Flugga
(Scotland)

The northernmost lighthouse in Scotland, Muckle Flugga, lies on a small rocky isle north of the Shetlands. It must be one of the most inhospitable places on earth – with almost constant storms, high waves and tides.

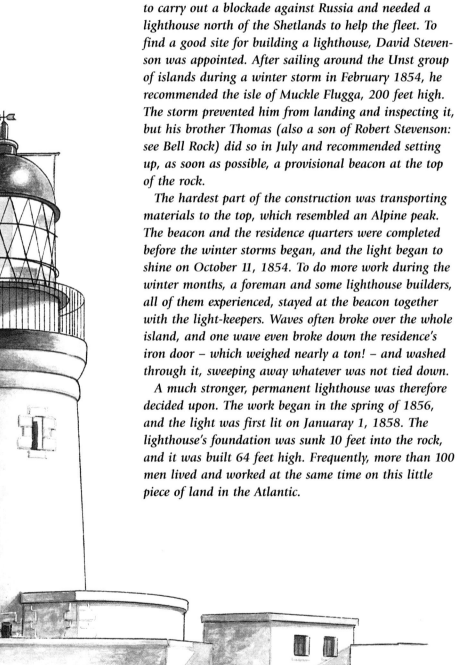

During the Crimean War in 1853-56, England wanted to carry out a blockade against Russia and needed a lighthouse north of the Shetlands to help the fleet. To find a good site for building a lighthouse, David Stevenson was appointed. After sailing around the Unst group of islands during a winter storm in February 1854, he recommended the isle of Muckle Flugga, 200 feet high. The storm prevented him from landing and inspecting it, but his brother Thomas (also a son of Robert Stevenson: see Bell Rock) did so in July and recommended setting up, as soon as possible, a provisional beacon at the top of the rock.

The hardest part of the construction was transporting materials to the top, which resembled an Alpine peak. The beacon and the residence quarters were completed before the winter storms began, and the light began to shine on October 11, 1854. To do more work during the winter months, a foreman and some lighthouse builders, all of them experienced, stayed at the beacon together with the light-keepers. Waves often broke over the whole island, and one wave even broke down the residence's iron door – which weighed nearly a ton! – and washed through it, sweeping away whatever was not tied down.

A much stronger, permanent lighthouse was therefore decided upon. The work began in the spring of 1856, and the light was first lit on Januaray 1, 1858. The lighthouse's foundation was sunk 10 feet into the rock, and it was built 64 feet high. Frequently, more than 100 men lived and worked at the same time on this little piece of land in the Atlantic.

Flannan Isles (Scotland)

In the Atlantic west of the outer Hebrides is a little, inaccessible island group named the Flannan Isles, or Seven Hunters. Nowadays all these isles are uninhabited except for large colonies of seabirds. But once they had a great religious importance, and those who landed on them were first required to pray for protection from misfortune. Many old tales are also recounted of a Saint Flann who lived in the isles.

Here the brothers David A. and Charles Stevenson (sons of David Stevenson: see Muckle Flugga) were appointed to build a lighthouse. The highest point on the isles is 285 feet above sea level, and at this place the construction began in 1895. The lighthouse was 75 feet high and its light was first lit on December 7, 1899. While the work may not have been very hard, it was an enormous task to bring all the materials, land them and transport them up to the site.

Late in 1900, something quite strange must have happened on the lighthouse island. A ship passed by on December 15, but the light was not shining. Soon it was time to change the personnel at the lighthouse and, on December 26, the light-keepers' boat came out with a new crew. Before going ashore, they noticed that something was wrong: no people were visible, no flag was raised, and no boxes stood on the quay for transport to the mainland. The captain blew a steam-whistle and signal rockets were fired, but there was no response on the isle. They disembarked and went up to the lighthouse. All was in good order at the residence house and the light – except that old, cold food lay on the kitchen table.

The whole island was searched, but none of the three light-keepers could be found. After a few days, however, damaged objects were discovered high up on the island, and some materials had been scattered all over it. Four men were left to tend the light, and the search continued, yet nothing more was found. Wild rumours circulated about how the three missing men had vanished – for example, that one of them had murdered the other two, thrown their bodies into the sea, and then drowned himself. It has never been possible to prove what happened, but a likely theory is that all of the light-keepers were working down at the landing quay and were suddenly hit by great waves, which swept them out to sea.

Fastnet Rock
(Ireland)

The rock of Fastnet, about 8 kilometres off Ireland's south-west coast, consists of two cliffs divided by a channel 8 metres wide. The highest cliff rises 26 metres above the sea, and legend tells that the Devil himself, when he was angry, took a piece of a mountain from the mainland and threw it into the ocean as an obstacle to seafarers. This cliff is also the first thing one sees when sailing from across the Atlantic.

Many ships had been wrecked on the rock, so in 1848 it was finally decided to build a lighthouse there, made of cast iron. The work at this very exposed site was completed in 1854, but the light-keepers could be changed only about 12 times per year, due to the weather conditions and the tide. Consequently, the keepers might easily have to stay there for an extra month. After some years, it was realized that the lighthouse would not last for long, and in 1865 the foundation was strengthened. During a storm in 1881 the light's lens was damaged, and in 1891 a decision was taken to build an entirely new lighthouse of granite, on the more protected western side of the cliff. This project began in 1895, and the new light, 176 feet high, was lit in 1904. By then, a total of 2,074 granite blocks weighing 4,300 tons had been brought from the mainland.

Black Rock, Mayo (Ireland)

Black Rock is a very small, desolate, rocky island on Ireland's west coast. Whatever one does, it is virtually impossible to land there with a boat. The isle is about 230 feet high, and receives an average rainfall of 1.8 metres during 200 days per year. Most of the year is stormy there as well, and the island is usually surrounded by sea mist.

The island's first beacon, which is still used today, was lit on June 1, 1864. At that time, when no helicopters existed, the light-keepers who arrived in October could not, as a rule, be replaced until February/March the next year. Nevertheless, two keepers' families lived on this tiny isle with their children and some cattle.

Hook Head
(Ireland)

The beacon of Hook Head dates back to the fifth century, and is considered the oldest one in Ireland. A monk from Wales named Dubhan, who was seeking solitude, moved to Ireland and out to Hook Point, the headland where the lighthouse now stands. When he saw the fishermen struggling near the promontory with all its currents, tides, waves and reefs, he built a primitive beacon that they could sail by. The light was a fire in an iron basket, mounted on a mast. Every evening the monk climbed up the mast on a ladder with wood, coal and other fuel to make a fire, which he tended throughout the night. Many years later he was declared a saint, and he is now un-officially regarded as the patron saint of Ireland's lighthouse administration.

Additional monks migrated out to Hook Point, and a small community grew. The monks tended the beacon until the early 12th century, when the Normans built a stone tower at the place to defend the area. A fire was lit at the top of the tower, but was extinguished at times during wars. In 1245, most of the lighthouse that we see today was constructed, and it still contains medieval fireplaces. The light was not electrified until 1972, and in 1977 the last keeper's family left the lighthouse.

Cordouan (France)

From the Bay of Biscay, the broad mouth of the Gironde River on France's west coast leads to the city of Bordeaux. This has always been a very important centre for French wine exports. Merchants came from Spain during the 13th century to buy wine, but many of them were ship-wrecked on the reef at the southern end of the river estuary. When they threatened to stop the trade, a fire was lit on the reef to show ships the right way into the river. It was named Cordouan as an honour to the Spanish traders.

The authorities in Bordeaux began to charge fees from ships as payment for keeping the fire. This was the first use of beacon fees in the world, already in the 1200s. During the next century, the open fire on the ground was replaced by a fire in an iron basket, supported on a tower about 15 metres high. The fire was tended by a hermit who lived on the reef, but when he died the fire was no longer kept, and ships once more foundered on the reef.

In 1584, the French architect Louis de Foix, who among other things had designed and built the castle of Escorial in Spain, was appointed to create a real lighthouse at Cordouan. He constructed a round stone base, 41 metres in diameter, and on this he raised a beautiful, strong tower 37 metres high. The work took all of 27 years, and the light was first lit in 1611.

This was a magnificent lighthouse! One entered it through an impos-ing hall. Above the royal chamber was a chapel with a vaulted roof, pil-lars, mosaics, altar and elegant windows. Outside, the whole building was covered with pillars, columns, statues and other ornaments. Thus, the design had been dominated by the idea of producing a handsome edifice. But it meant that one could hardly see the light, a fire burning in an iron basket at the top of the tower.

In 1727, the lantern with all its stone columns was replaced by an iron structure. The iron basket and fire gave way to oil lamps, placed in front of reflectors. The old tower was heightened to 57 metres in 1789. Since then, the lighthouse's illumination has steadily been modernized. Yet the beautiful old lower section, with the royal chamber and the chapel, still exists and probably makes Cordouan the prettiest lighthouse in the world today.

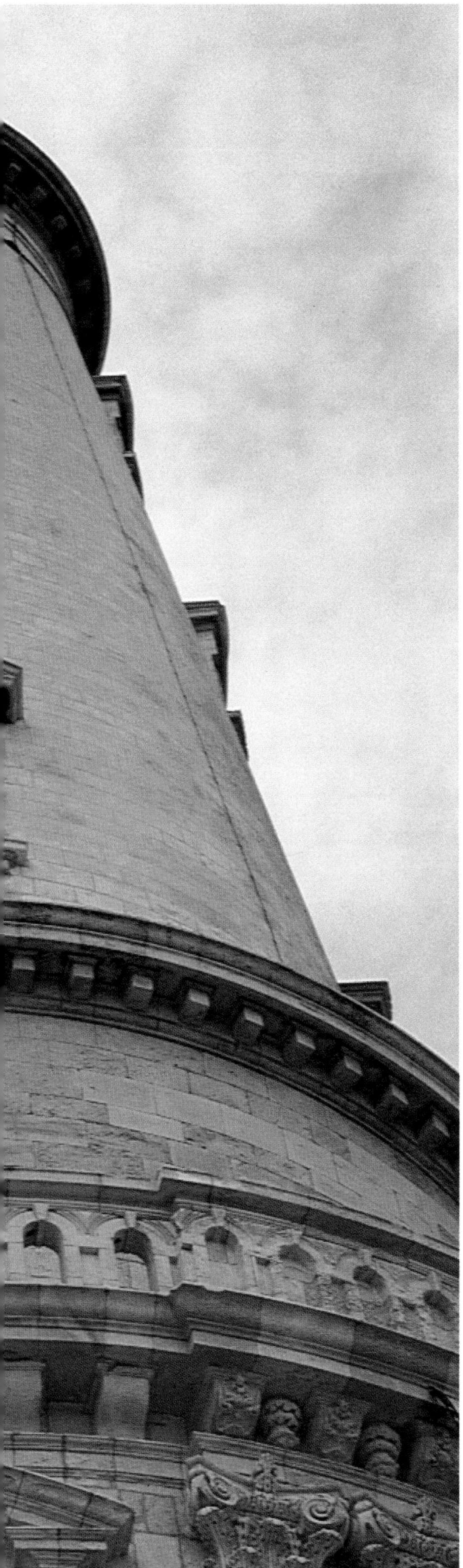

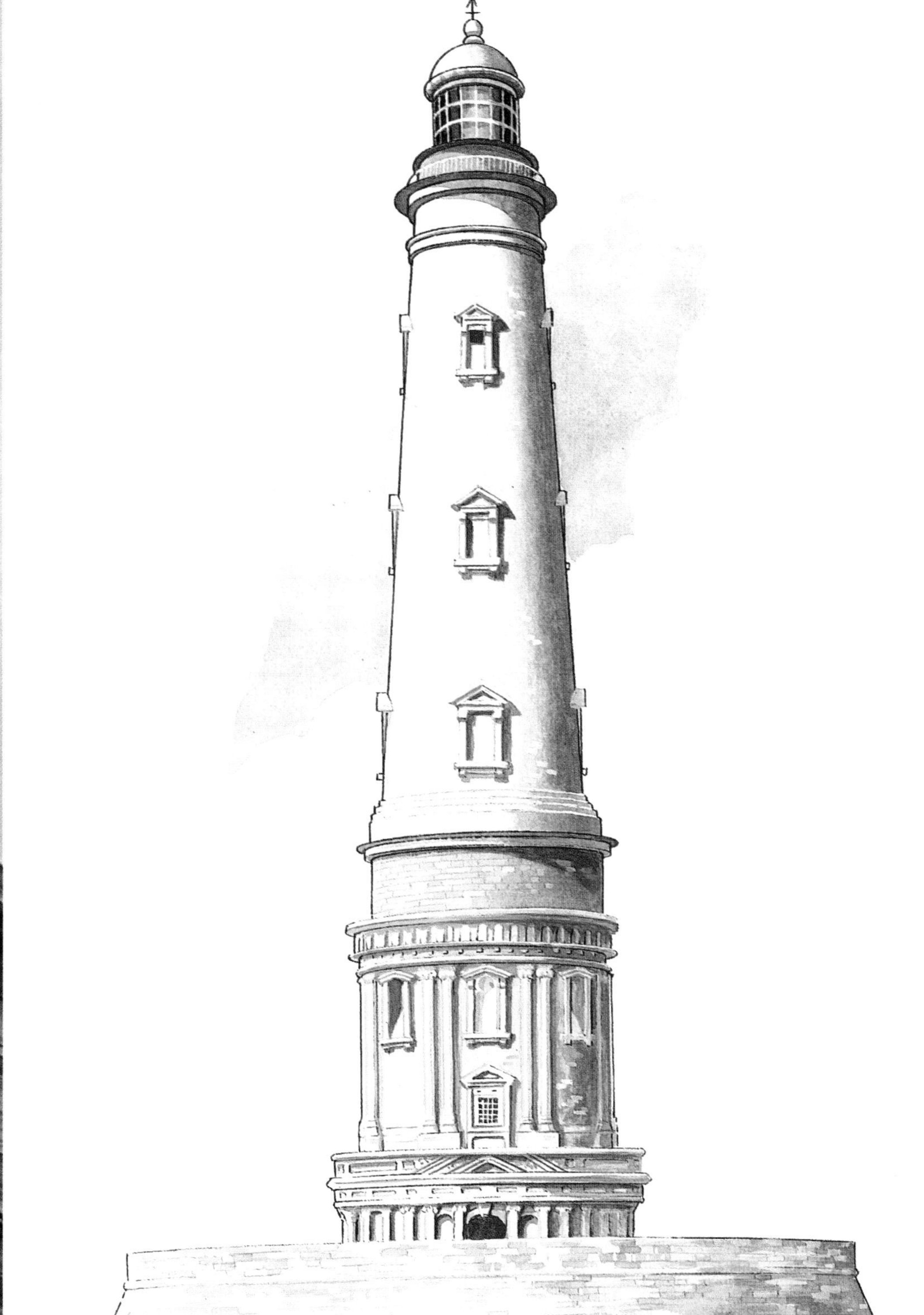

Ile Vierge (France)

On the little island of Vierge, near Brittany's north-west corner, was built the highest lighthouse in Europe – 82.5 metres – between the years 1897 and 1902.. This classic lighthouse continues to shine, and is made of granite. A short distance away lies its predecessor, a small beacon erected in 1845, which is now extinguished but still serves as an important seamark.

La Jument (France)

A relatively young lighthouse, La Jument lies on a small rock in the sea to the south of Ile de Quessant. Its construction began in 1904 but was not finished until 1911. Due to its exposed position, the work had to continue with reinforcement until as late as 1940. In the period when the lighthouse was manned, the French light-keepers regarded it as perhaps the most exposed and dangerous place for them to work.

Le Stiff (France)

On the cliffs at the northeast corner of Ile de Quessant, an island near Brittany, work began in 1695 to build the lighthouse which still operates there today. It is constructed with a unique double body, and is one of the oldest lighthouses in France.

Europe Point
(Gibraltar)

At the entrance to the Mediterranean Sea, on Europe Point in Gibraltar, is a lighthouse that was built by English army engineers in 1837-1841. This was natural, since Gibraltar served as an English fortress. The lighthouse, 19 metres high and standing 30 metres above sea level, was first lit in August 1841. But history tells us that already in 1492, some type of beacon at the same place existed to show the way for passing ships. Next to its light was a wooden statue of the Virgin Mary.

La Coruña (Spain)

This site is thought to have possessed a beacon ever since the third century. Like today's lighthouse, it stood on a hill about 60 metres above sea level, just outside the city of La Coruña. There is also a written description of Julius Caesar lying at anchor with his war fleet near the beacon.

The lighthouse is known, too, as the Tower of Hercules. According to legend, after Hercules had killed the giants, he buried their bones and built the beacon on the grave. In addition, the beacon was described in the 5th century as a point of orientation which the Romans were fortunate to use during their voyages to Brittany. A map from 1086 shows this beacon as well as the Pharos lighthouse at Alexandria.

Apparently the beacon fell into disrepair and was renovated at regular intervals. Finally, though, a thorough reconstruction was made between 1785 and 1790 on the initiative of King Carlos III. Except for its technical lighting equipment, the lighthouse looks the same today as it did after the work in 1790.

Porto Pi (Spain)

Among Spain's oldest light-houses is the one at Porto Pi, on the southwest coast of Majorca. At first, in 1290, a simple tower was built to hold some kind of light. But during the 17th century, a fort was constructed around this beacon, and the glass in its lantern broke when the fort's cannon were fired. Therefore, the light was moved to an adjacent sig-nal-tower that had been built at the same time as the original tower.

Guia *(Portugal)*

Lighthouses in Portugal have a relatively short history which began at Porto, the well-known city that is most famous for its far-reaching trade in port wine. None of these 18th-century lighthouses has survived, but the next oldest one in the country is Guia, on the high promontory west of Lisbon. This finely preserved and beautiful eight-sided tower was erected in 1771, and is 28 metres high. As at most other lighthouses in Portugal, the lantern at Guia is entirely French-built. Previously it was called Nossa Senhora Guia (Our Lady of Guia), but today it is called simply Guia.

Bugio *(Portugal)*

Outside Lisbon, southeast of the River Teijo's estuary, is the lighthouse of Bugio. Built in 1755 at the older fort of San Lourenço da Barra, it stands on a reef and has been hard-pressed by the waves during the years. In 1755 the fort, which had a diameter of 50 metres and a circuit wall no less than 150 metres across, was struck by a tidal wave after a serious earthquake. Later that year, it was decided to erect a lighthouse in the middle of the fort, to warn seafarers away from the dangerous reef. But the original lighthouse is gone, as the fort decayed so much that a decision was taken in 1896 to replace both the fort and the lighthouse. The new light shines from a height of 28 metres and was automated in 1981.

Livorno *(Italy)*

Already in 1154 the Republic of Pisa erected the first lighthouse in this part of Italy (at Meloria). It was destroyed by the Genoese army during a war in 1284, but replaced in 1304 by a new lighthouse at Livorno. The latter was ruined in World War II and reconstructed in 1956, using material from the old lighthouse.

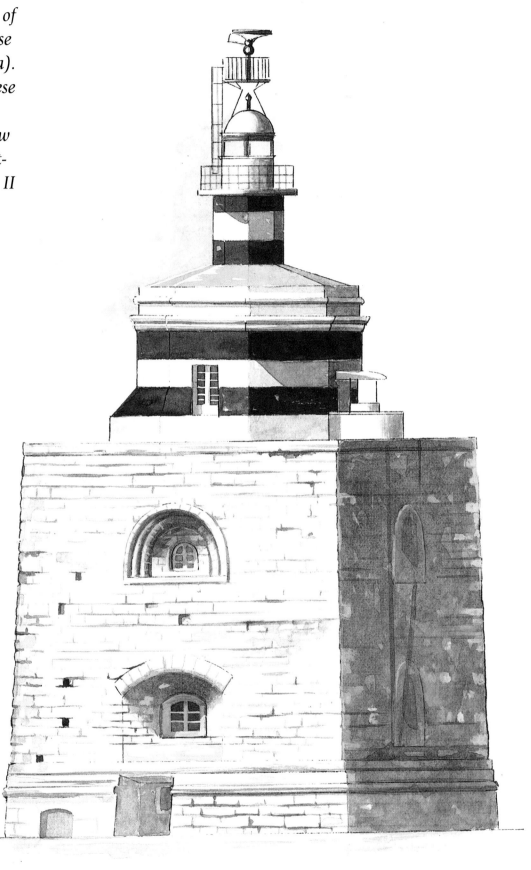

La Lanterna, Genoa
(Italy)

Possibly no other country contains as many old lighthouse towers as Italy. Their illumination has naturally been modernized, but numerous examples were partly or entirely built between the 13th and 16th centuries.

The best-known Italian lighthouse may be La Lanterna in Genoa, which dates back to 1161. An interesting detail is that Antonio Colombo, the uncle of Christopher Columbus, is said to have been its keeper in 1449. However, the lighthouse was in such poor condition by 1543 that the contemporary Genoese Republic built a completely new lighthouse. This is used today and has a tower 76 metres high, with a lantern at 117.5 metres above the sea.

Lista (Norway)

The lighthouse of Lista stands on one of Norway's southern-most capes. Already at the end of the 18th century it was proposed to build a beacon there. This did not begin until the spring of 1834, and the granite beacon, 34 metres high, was lit on November 10, 1836. Distinctive light characters did not exist at the time, and in 1843 it was proposed to build two more identical beacons at the place, to make a visible difference from other lights. The work began in 1851 and on September 16, 1853, three lights at once were lit on Lista for the first time. It was among the very few sites in the world to have three beacons. The personnel numbered no fewer than seven, which was probably a contemporary record. In 1873, after light characters had been created, a new lens apparatus was installed in the northern-most beacon. The other two beacons were removed, to be set up on Svenner in 1874 and Haltens in 1875.

Færder (Norway)

On the island of Stora Færder in the outskirts of Oslo Fjord, a simple beacon was established already in 1697. It consisted of a fire in an iron basket laid directly on the ground atop a hill about 35 metres above the sea. Moreover, a small house was built for the fire-tender and a shed for the wood. The beacon was owned by a private individual who, in return, was allowed to take beacon fees from passing ships. The profits were maximized by saving on fuel, so the light became weak and unreliable.

In 1796 the famous Danish captain Paul Løvenørn was made chief of the pilotage administration in Denmark and Norway. He thought a proper beacon should be erected at the place. When the old beacon's owner refused to invest more money, the site was taken over by the state in 1799, and a new coal-fired beacon of stone was built with a lantern. This light was first kindled on May 2, 1802. In 1852, it was abolished and replaced by a first-order lens light, which had been built of iron next to the old beacon. Two years later, the light was moved to the island of Tristein (Lilla Færder), where it was first lit on July 1, 1857. The old foundation of the stone beacon, which was one of Norway's oldest beacons, still exists on Stora Færder.

Skagen *(Denmark)*

Denmark was the first Scandinavian country to establish large sea lights and coastal lighthouses (at Falsterbo in 1202, Skagen and Anholt and Kullen in 1560, Nidingen in 1624, Læsø in 1651). At Skagen, the oldest example was what is called a parrot beacon (its appearance is not certain today, but it probably resembled the swape light that was designed afterward). A bit later, this was replaced by a wooden tower with tallow lamps. When it became possible to buy coal from England, Jens Pedersen Grove invented the light that is known as a swape – with coal in an uplifted iron basket. The first swape was erected in 1627 at Skagen. In 1747, however, it gave way to a coal fire in a stone tower, which in turn was replaced in 1858 by the existing stone beacon, 46 metres high.

Anholt (Denmark)

Almost the same development as Skagen's occurred at Anholt: first a parrot beacon, then a wooden one with tallow lamps, in about 1630 a swape, in 1788 a stone tower 30 metres high with an open coal fire, and in 1809 a closed coal beacon. The tower was extended in 1881, when a lens light was added. Today, the tower is 42 metres high. During the Napoleonic War in 1809-14, the beacon was occupied by the English, who built a fort around it.

Nidingen (Sweden)

Sweden got its first beacon, on the isle of Nidingen, as war booty from Denmark in 1645, by the Treaty of Brömsebro when the county of Halland and other regions were acquired. The beacon was built by the Danes in 1624 as a coal-fired, open light. At that time there were no lights with different characters, so it was hard for sailors to distinguish between the Danish lights in the Kattegat straits. Consequently, in 1629 the old light of Nidingen was replaced by two coal-fired swape lights, which made Nidingen the world's first double beacon.

Today, those lights have gone out of use and Nidingen has a modern light from 1946. The former beacons were built in 1832, of stone from the fortress of Varberg, and were extended in 1846. Since then, they have not been changed but only maintained as historic buildings. In 1766 on Nidingen, the world's first manned fog-signal station was erected, consisting of a metal bell hung in a tower. In 1873, two cannons were also installed as fog signals. The fog bell was moved in 1886 to the beacon site of Böttö, outside Gothenburg, and in 1946 to the city's Maritime Museum. One of the cannons still lies on Nidingen.

Vinga (Sweden)

Probably the most renowned lighthouse in Sweden, and the one which is first seen from a ship approaching Swedish waters from the west, is Vinga outside Gothenburg. Built relatively late, in 1841, it became the first Swedish lighthouse to be equipped with a Fresnel lens apparatus. But this lighthouse was replaced in 1856 by a new one. In 1890 it was demolished and replaced by the present lighthouse, while the original one was rebuilt as a pilot lookout.

Since Vinga was an important approach point on the Swedish coast, though, the island had a red-painted seamark already in about 1765. This gave way in 1720 to a pyramid-shaped wooden tower with a lookout. The latter burned down in the mid-1800s, and in 1854 the legendary beacon that we see today was erected.

Landsort (Sweden)

A beacon was established on Landsort already in 1642. Next, the isle acquired the first lighthouse in Sweden that was built by Swedes themselves. It was first lit in 1669, but being made of wood, it burned down in 1672, so an open coal beacon was constructed of stone. In 1840, a new lantern was added with a mirror apparatus to strengthen the light. The original tower was rebuilt through the years, until 1870 when it received its present appearance.

Grundkallen (Sweden)

The first caisson beacon in the open sea, at Rothersand, was built by the Germans as early as 1885. Constructing the upper part of such a beacon on the site could be very complicated, so Robert Gellerstad in Sweden developed a telescopic caisson beacon – patented in 1957 – which was built completely in a harbour and then towed out to the site, sunk to the bottom and anchored. Then the finished superstructure was raised telescopically, and the beacon was more or less ready for operation.

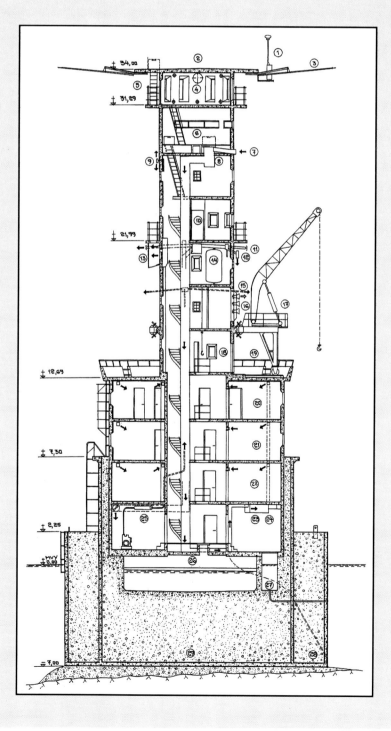

Grundkallen was the first large Swedish telescopic beacon. Its construction, on the isle of Lidingö outside Stockholm, began on January 31, 1958. After becoming probably the only Swedish beacon in history to be blessed by a priest, it was launched on June 7, 1958. Some additional work followed, and then started a quite complex operation of towing the heavy "ship" out to its site on the Dittman shoal, where it was sunk to the bottom and made ready. Grundkallen was also the first Swedish beacon to be provided with a helicopter platform. By 1972, all Swedish lightships had been replaced by telescopic caisson beacons.

1	Hoistable radar antenna
2	Helideck (helicopter landing pad)
3	8 communications antennas
4	Lights and lenses
5	Stairs to helideck
6	Upper watch room
7	Fresh air intake
8	Water condensation tanks
9	Ventilation pipes for sewage system
10	Lower watch room
11	Chimney
12	Ventilation pipes for oil tanks
13	Ventilation pipes for machine rooms and living accommodations
14	Pressured air tanks
15	Exhaust pipe for diesel engine
16	Tyfon (fog signal)
17	Derrick
18	Main entrance
19	Derrick and entrance deck
20	Offices, bedrooms, kitchen, dining and living room, lavatory
21	Bedrooms, bathrooms, storage rooms, lavatories
22	Bedrooms (spare ones), storage rooms, laundry room, hobby room, air conditioning system, etc.
23	Storage rooms for batteries used as reserve for ventilation and heating
24	Heat exchanging system
25	Machine room, boiler room, workshop and oil storage tanks
26	Fresh water tanks
27	Salt water intake
28	Lightning conductor and earth connection for telecommunication
29	Caisson

Bogskär (Finland)

Bogskär is an original Finnish lighthouse, built in 1880 of iron on a lonely little skerry in the Baltic Sea. When erected, it was called Finland's Eddystone because of the exposed location. During a hard winter storm in 1889, for example, the waves and ice swept away all building materials and all the storehouses. The lighthouse's lower part was damaged so much that it nearly collapsed into the water. This site is very isolated from the world, and during the 1890s the light-keepers' only contact was by carrier pigeon with Åland, but in 1908 wireless telegraphy was introduced. The oldest lighthouse has now been replaced by a modern one.

Kopu *(Estonia)*

This unique, massive white lighthouse was constructed of limestone in 1531. As a national monument, it is protected for the future. It may not seem beautiful with its broad, upward-tapering supports built into a square body, but it definitely looks powerful.

Rozewie *(Poland)*

It is believed that some sort of beacon has existed at this place since the Middle Ages, and already in 1696 the beacon was marked on Swedish sea charts. The present-day lighthouse was first lit on November 15, 1822, and has been rebuilt several times, as well as raised twice because the surrounding coastal forest has grown ever higher. On the lighthouse, one can also see clearly where the extensions of the tower have been made. This lighthouse is a very significant historical monument in Poland.

Arkona
(Germany)

In the northern part of the island of R¸gen are two lighthouses, almost next to each other. Both are registered as buildings of historical interest. The oldest, a four-sided brick structure with a round lantern, was first lit in 1827. It was replaced in 1902 by the present lighthouse, built of bricks like an ordinary round tower. The older lighthouse now holds a maritime museum.

Neuwerk
(Germany)

On an island in the estuary of the River Elbe, Neuwerk is the oldest German lighthouse still in operation. Its four-sided building dates from 1310, but the light was not installed at its top until 1814.

Bremerhaven
(Germany)

No fewer than twelve lighthouses stand around the city of Bremerhaven, and they all look very different. The oldest one is named Bremerhaven and was lit in 1854. Its tower, 37 metres high, is made of red bricks and has a Gothic design, resembling a church tower and beautifully ornamented with pillars and decorative windows. The architect who designed it was also responsible for the city's main church. On one side of the tower is an iron arm, where storm-warning signals were once raised.

Terschelling Brandaris
(Holland)

Two simple beacons stood already in 1280 at the mouth of the River Maas. During the 16th century, more beacons began to be built, for example at Terschelling and Goeree. On a church tower at Brandaris in 1593, a fire beacon was established and continued in use until the 1750s.

Robben Island (South Africa)

Tiny Robben Island lies in the bay outside Cape Town, ten kilometres north of the lighthouse at Green Point. As early as the 17th century, it was used as a prison and later also as a leper colony. The island is also where South Africa's president Nelson Mandela was imprisoned for many years.

In 1862 the construction of a lighthouse started at the island's highest point, where South Africa's first fire beacon had also been lit in 1656. The lighthouse was 60 feet high and equipped with a first-order lens made by Chance Brothers in England. It began to shine on January 1, 1865, and continues in operation today.

Green Point
(South Africa)

According to old records, a signal fire for sailors was established already in 1656 on Robben Island, outside Cape Town. The first real lighthouse in South Africa, how-ever, is considered to be the one whose construction began in 1821.

South Africa was then a colony of the British and, as elsewhere in their empire, the building of light-houses had to be approved by the government in London. When the work started, it soon had to stop, as the necessary permit had not been acquired. But agreement was reached on the great need for a lighthouse to help all the ships that rounded the cape, so permission was granted. The light was first lit on April 12, 1824, and is still in use. It became very important for South Africa, and was also used as a training centre for non-white light-keepers.

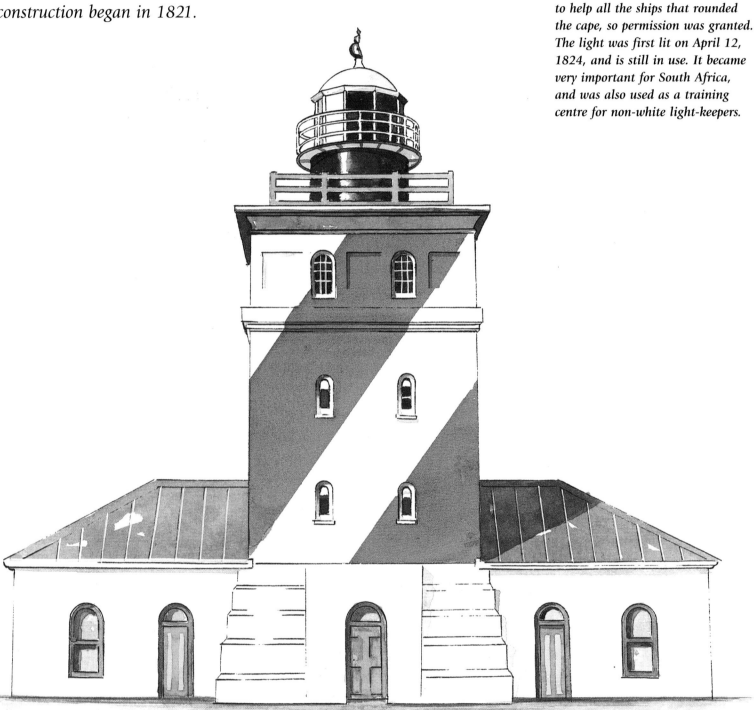

Cape Agulhas *(South Africa)*

Cape Agulhas is the southernmost tip of the African continent. Its name is Portuguese and means the tip of a compass needle, which was once believed to spin wildly when one rounded this cape. The cape is surrounded by dangerous reefs and was terrifying to sailors. After long discussion with the British government, it was decided to build South Africa's fourth lighthouse here. The light was first lit on March 1, 1849, and is still used. It has shown the way for countless seafarers on voyages around Africa.

Minicoy *(India)*

Far out at sea, off the southwest coast of India, lie the Minicoy Islands. They became very important due to their strategic position for seafaring when the Suez Canal was opened in 1869. To help ships find the islands, a beacon was built there between 1883 and 1885. India was then a British colony, so the lighthouse was controlled by England's administration at Trinity House. While India gained independence in 1947, the lighthouse did not pass into Indian hands until 1963. But in practical terms, India took it over already in 1956, when the Indian flag replaced the English one on the islands.

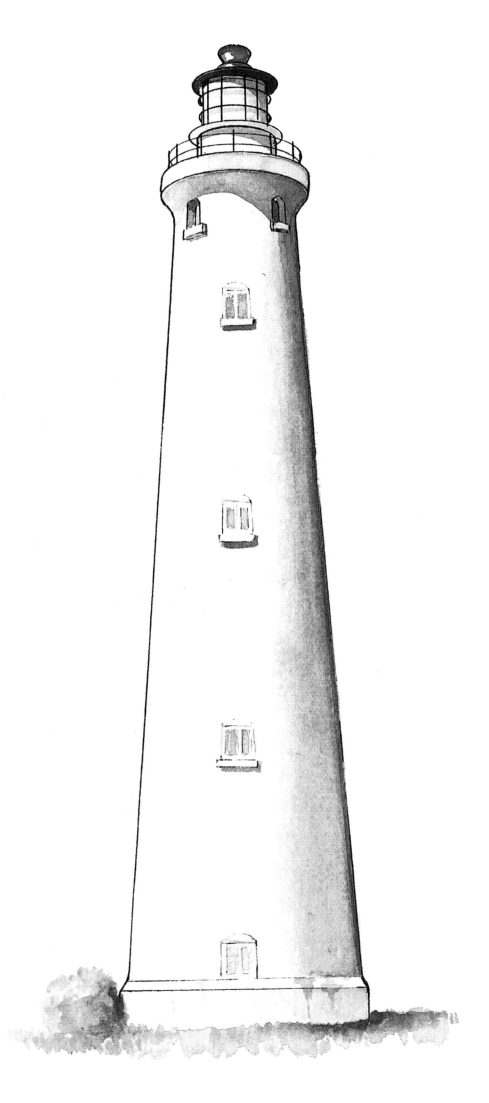

Horsburgh
(Singapore)

Singapore has only five light-houses, the oldest being Hors-burgh which began to shine in 1851. Lying on the small, lonely rock of Pedra Branca ("white rock"), it marks the eastern entrance to the Singapore Straits from the South China Sea. Before the lighthouse was built, hundreds of ships were wrecked on this rock.

Jingxin Pagodas
(China)

The Chinese feel that their old pagodas should also be regarded as some kind of lighthouse, since these have been used as seamarks for many centuries. In the harbour of the city of Wenzhou are two such pagodas, built in 869 and 969 respectively. According to legend, they have always been used as lights in line, and today they perform the same service.

Macquarie Lighthouse *(Australia)*

General Lachlan Macquarie, the governor of Australia's state of New South Wales during 1810-21, decided that the country's first lighthouse should be built at South Head, on the southern side of the entrance to Sydney harbour (then called Port Jackson). Although Australia was an English colony, the lighthouse was erected without official approval from England, and was lit on November 30, 1818. Its designer and constructor was an architect who, like so many other people in Australia at the time, had been imprisoned and exiled from England. After a couple of years, the sandstone tower began to crumble apart, and had to be held together with iron bands. Eventually these became so numerous that the need for a new lighthouse was realized. The second tower was an exact copy, built next to the old one. It was lit on June 1, 1883, and then the old one was destroyed.

When the decision was taken to build the second lighthouse, the Prime Minister of New South Wales mentioned in a speech that, when the old one was erected, only 20,000 Europeans had lived in the colony and only 4-5,000 of them were free men, the rest being condemned prisoners. Now there were 750,000 Europeans, so a new and better lighthouse was essential.

Cape Wickham
(Australia)

The tallest lighthouse tower in Australia, at Cape Wickham, is 48 metres high. It stands on King Island in Bass Strait, north of Tasmania. This strait was, and still is, a very exposed and dangerous passage for the sea-faring between Australia and Tasmania. For no less than 20 years, it was discussed which place in the strait would be most suitable before the light-house's construction began. It was ready to be lit in 1861, and became automatic already in 1918.

Pencarrow Head
(New Zealand)

The first lighthouse in New Zealand was not lit until January 1, 1859. It stood on Pencarrow Head, at the entrance to Wellington's harbour. As New Zealand was then an English colony, most lighthouses were prefabricated in England and shipped out to be assembled at their sites. This initial lighthouse, also made in England, was of iron – transported in 480 packets weighing a total of 60 tons, on the vessel Ambrosire which reached New Zealand in June 1858. The country's lighthouses tend to be relatively short, as they normally stand high above the sea. Pencarrow Head itself was 98 metres high, but had constant problems with low clouds, which meant that the light could not always be seen. Consequently, in 1906, another lighthouse was built lower down. The original one is now a seamark and a historic building.

Mikomoto-Shima
(Japan)

The oldest Japanese stone-built lighthouse that is still active, Mikomoto-Shima, was first lit in 1870. Like nearly all the lighthouses erected in Japan during the 19th century, it was designed by an Englishman, Richard Brunton. Since Japan opened up to foreign ships at the end of the century, many lighthouses were constructed at just that time.

Cape Florida Light (USA)

A beacon tower 65 metres high was built in 1825 at Cape Florida, which then lay in the midst of an area inhabited by Seminole Indians. The Indians were tired of unfulfilled promises from the white men and gave constant battle. Thus on July 23, 1836, the tower was attacked by a large band of Indians, but the light-keeper and his assistant got safely inside and closed the door. During the rifle fire back and forth, the Indians shot holes in a tank containing oil for the beacon light. The oil began to burn and the tower door caught fire, so the two men fled higher up, but the fire spread upward along the wooden stairs. At last the whole tower was engulfed in flames, and the men huddled outside on the red-hot iron lantern while the Indians shot at them. The assistant was killed, but a naval ship arrived in the nick of time and saved the keeper.

The destroyed tower was repaired, but not lit again until 1846. Some years later, it was heightened to 100 metres and given a lens apparatus. Yet doom struck once more in 1861, during the Civil War. The Confederate army wrecked the lens apparatus, and the light could not be relit until 1866. It kept shining for 12 years, and was then replaced by a lighthouse at another site. In the 1970s, the US Coast Guard decided to repair the original beacon, and this was relit in 1978 when it reached the age of exactly 100.

Cape Hatteras (USA)

The best-known lighthouse in America is probably that at Cape Hatteras, in the long chain of islands outside North Carolina on the east coast. These are low sandy isles, very exposed to wind and waves, which undermine everything that is built on the shores. They are called the cemetery of the Atlantic, as about 2,500 ships have been wrecked there since the early 16th century.

The first lighthouse, 95 feet high, was given 18 oil lamps with reflectors and became operational in October 1803. But there were complaints that it could not be seen at sea, and in 1854 it was heightened to 150 feet. In 1863, a first-order Fresnel lens was added. Throughout the years, reinforcements were necessary in the foundation, since the ocean and the sand continually threatened to overturn the tower.

As the complaints about its visibility persisted, a new lighthouse 193 feet high was built. Made of brick, it is probably the tallest brick tower in America. The light was lit in 1870 and still remains in the same place. But the shore erosion has proceeded and, after decades of discussion, it was decided in 1998 to move the whole lighthouse farther up on land, so that it would not collapse some day.

Boston Harbor Light
(USA)

The first lighthouse that was built in North America – and thus also in the United States – was the Boston Harbor Light, on Little Brewster Island outside the city of Boston at the northeast coast. Older than the American nation itself, this lighthouse was built in 1716 by the little English colony in Massachusetts. Following European fashion, it was financed by the beacon fees that were charged on ships entering Boston's harbour. It had a glass lantern and the light consisted of tallow lamps. In 1719, a large cannon was added, for signalling in fog. The cannon is preserved at the US Coast Guard Academy in New London.

The American Revolution left the lighthouse in ruins, and in 1783 it was decided to build a new one. This was first lit in 1789, and still exists. In 1859, the tower was extended to the present height and, at the same time, a second-order Fresnel lens was installed, which is also still there. The Boston Harbor Light is the only American lighthouse that continues to be manned – and according to the law, it must stay manned in the future.

Colonia del Sacramento
(Uruguay)

In January 1855, the lighthouse at Colonia del Sacramento was first lit. It lies in the oldest quarter of the city with the same name. The old buildings around the lighthouse are listed as a world heritage site by UNESCO.

Santo Antonio
(Brazil)

This lighthouse lies within the walls of Brazil's oldest fort. It was the first lighthouse to be constructed on the American continent, and began to shine in December 1698.

Index

Lighthouses on pages 116-187